P9-CCS-959

# HOW TO FEEL A REAL GOLF SWING

# HOW TO FEEL A REAL GOLF SWING

By Bob Toski and Davis Love, Jr.
With Robert Carney

Illustrations by Elmer Wexler

Random House

Published by Golf Digest/Tennis, Inc., and Random House, Inc.

Golf Digest/Tennis, Inc.
A New York Times Company
5520 Park Avenue Box 395
Trumbull, Conn. 06611-0395

Random House, Inc.
201 East 50th Street
New York, N.Y. 10022

First printing 1988
Manufactured in the United States of America
98765432

Library of Congress Cataloging-in-Publication Data

Toski, Bob.
How to feel a real golf swing / Bob Toski and Davis Love, Jr; with Robert Carney; illustrations by Elmer Wexler. p. cm.

ISBN 0-394-56121-X

1. Swing (Golf) I. Love, Davis II. Carney, Robert, 1945- . III. Title.
GV979.S9T596 1987 796.352' 3—dc 19 87-28351 CIP

# CONTENTS

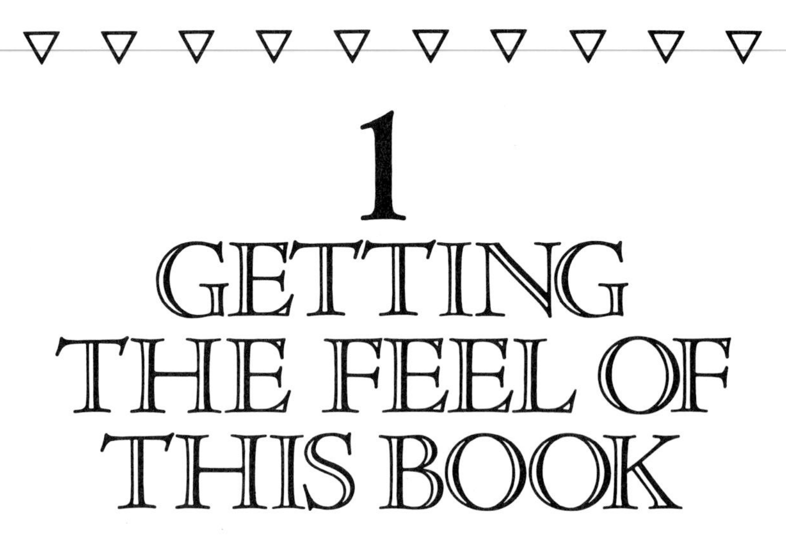

# 1 GETTING THE FEEL OF THIS BOOK

Imagine that you are sitting in a park. It is a lovely summer day, warm enough for shirt sleeves but just breezy enough to keep cool and comfortable. Fifty yards away a mother watches her daughter in a swing. The child is 7 or 8, just discovering the joys of the swing. At first she kicks and pulls herself jerkily, only a few feet in either direction, but as she gains confidence she gives herself to the motion of the swing, tucking her feet in as she falls back down, kicking her shoes forward to reach as high as she can going up. Soon she is soaring, backward and forward, to a point almost as high as the crossbar. The chains that connect the swing to the crossbar bow slightly as she reaches the apex in either direction, while the creak of the swing seat keeps her time.

The little girl is free, at peace, delighted to feel this constant, rhythmic motion.

If only a golf swing could be as easy and natural, could feel as good! We think it can. We believe that when you feel the freedom and rhythm of the proper swinging motion for yourself, you will never lose it; you will realize, like the little girl, that surrender to that swinging motion is the ultimate control and the key to DISTANCE and ACCURACY.

In the Golf Digest Schools we do an exercise. Bob or Davis will ask a student to toss a ball at an outstretched hand. Nine times out of 10 the student will hit the hand with the ball on the first throw. It's uncanny how accurate students are. Then Davis will say, "That was pretty good. But how would you like to do better?" "Oh sure," the student says. And Davis will say, "OK, this time make a small backswing with your wrist before you start to throw the ball, then get your arm into it. As you're about to release the ball, repeat that sequence. Move the arm first and then flip the ball with the wrist. Hold it lightly. Now, go."

If that second ball comes within five feet of us it's a miracle. By then we've filled that student's brain so full of mechanical thoughts that he's completely lost the feel of his throw.

But isn't that exactly how most of us learn to play golf? When was the last time you played a round with no "self-instruction" about how to hit the ball right? "Don't let the right elbow fly." "Don't let the club get 'outside.'" "Don't sway." "Don't reverse pivot." "Don't leave your weight on your right side." And on and on until on the 18th hole your only thought is, "I'm going to quit this game."

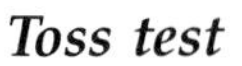

***Toss test***
*If filling your head full of mechanical thoughts can sabotage an act as simple as tossing a ball, it can ruin your golf swing.*

## A "Do" book

This book is an escape from the "Don't" quagmire. It is a book of "Do's," presented not as rigid commandments but as guides to feeling the motion—underline motion—of the swing. It recognizes that sound mechanics are essential to a good golf swing, but that you learn mechanics in several ways. You learn by Reading (or hearing), by Observing and by Feeling the movement for yourself. For example, you might read a book on hitting by baseball-great Ted Williams and try to do what Williams says. Or, you might go out to the ballpark and watch batting practice and try to copy the swings you see. Finally, you might play a game of "pepper" with your friends to capture the feeling of proper timing in hitting ball with bat.

In our experience, Reading (or merely hearing) instruction is the least effective of the three. Our toss test proves that. Observing is better. Even if our student had never tossed a ball, he would quickly learn how to do it by watching Davis toss the ball to him. When the action gets more complicated than tossing a ball, however, the best method is Feel. Remember when you learned to ride a bike? Instructions were almost worthless. Watching your brother or sister do it helped a lot. But until you got the feel of balancing yourself on that two-wheeler, even watching wasn't enough. Once you got the feel, it was impossible to forget.

We think the easiest way to learn to play golf is the way you learned to ride that bike. By instinct, by feel. We know that if we can help you learn that way, you will learn to swing the club, not maneuver it. We know that if you learn to feel that clubhead swinging, you'll find the tempo, the pace, the rhythm that's right for you.

That's not to say that we'll ignore reading or seeing as methods of learning. This book will give you all three with a decided emphasis on feel. It will explain how the golf swing happens. It will show you, in illustrations, the proper movements within the swing. But most of all, it will give you the exercises to capture the feel of those movements for good.

## Learning by feel

Many teachers ignore feel. They don't trust a student's instincts. They put him in positions and then tell him to move his body and the club until he achieves those positions. The great teachers—Ernest Jones, Percy Boomer, Henry Cotton, Harvey Penick (who taught both Tom Kite

and Ben Crenshaw) and, of course, Bob Toski—know that golf is a motion game and that positions are only an early stepping stone to creating that motion. They trust your instincts to help you create a swing that fits you, a swing that you'll be able to ingrain and repeat.

Because this book is different, we ask you to be different as you use it. This is a hands-on book, a workbook or, better yet, a playbook. It's a book you lay on the floor while you try one of our exercises. It's a book we think you will keep around for a long time—there's no hurry about learning the golf swing.

On the other hand, it's a book you can "graduate" from. Once you've learned a particular movement through feel, you've got it. You can move on.

We liken this book to the old Arthur Murray dance lessons Davis sent away for as a shy and awkward teenager in El Dorado, Ark. One day they arrived with a fold-up

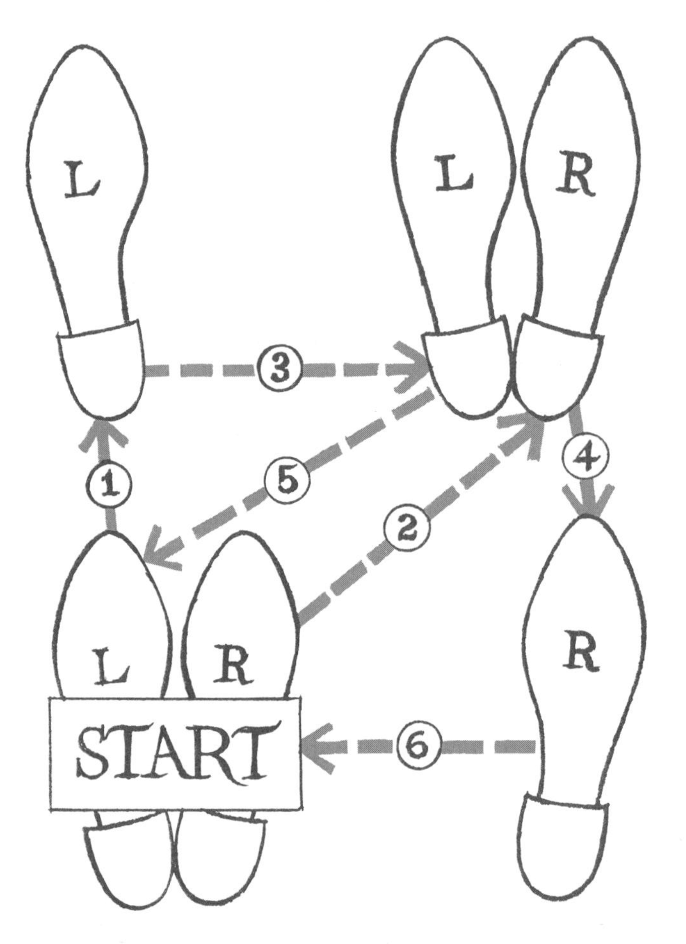


***Davis' diagrams***
*Learn to swing the way Davis learned to dance. First, master the positions, then swing to the music within you.*

diagram of the fox-trot steps. "I read the instructions," says Davis. "Then, with the door to my bedroom closed and locked, I laid the diagram on the floor, placed my feet on the steps marked 'Start' and walked through it. Still following instructions, I walked through again, this time with an even rhythm. Next, I turned on the Victrola and walked through to the beat of the music. And finally, after lots of walk-throughs with the door still closed, I danced. Danced! I didn't need diagrams or words or walk-throughs. Never again."

## The music within you

The music of the golf swing is within you. To discover it, however, you'll need to do what Davis did. Learn to feel it, one step at a time. We have arranged the chapters so that the earliest ones provide the greatest payoffs. It's fine to skip around, but you'll improve more quickly if you follow the chapters in order. We've organized the book by body parts, with the most critical parts coming first, the early chapters providing foundation for later ones.

There are three kinds of exercises. Those done without the club, those done with the club but without the ball and those done hitting the ball with the club. You wouldn't think of teaching your children to ride a bike before they had learned to balance themselves on their feet. The no-ball exercises make the driving-range exercises easy. We've provided a suggested "game plan" at the end of each chapter to help you order your practice.

Do all the exercises and do them in the order the game plans suggest. A tip: The exercises that you find hardest to do are probably the ones that will deliver the biggest benefits. Make a game out of them. If you're trying to touch the grips of two clubs together, for example, establish a personal best and try to better it.

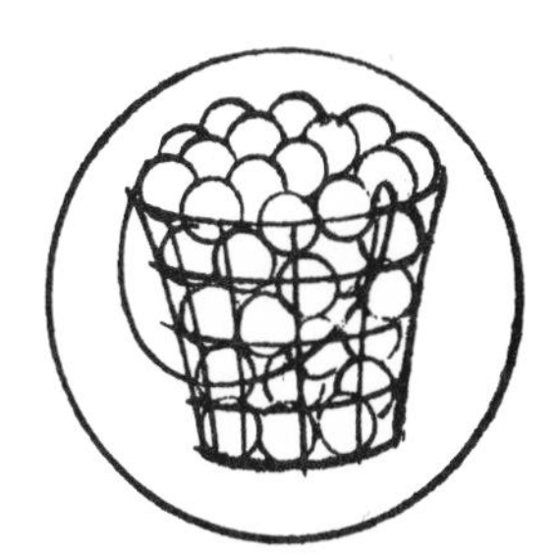

You'll also master the exercises quickest if you take each one in three stages: First, concentrate on learning the exercise movement with no thought about results. Then, once you've mastered the movement, be attentive to how it feels. Finally, concentrate on your result, whether it be the number of repetitions you're doing with a no-ball exercise or the kind of shot you're trying to hit with a ball. If we ask you to imagine, for example, that you are "flinging the club away" as you hit balls, don't be satisfied that your shots are relatively solid. Your first goal is to swing the club as if you

were flinging it. Your second goal is to feel that motion. Your third goal is to hit good shots using it.

Once you master a particular movement, you've got it. Two months from now you won't have to go back and say, "What did they say about the hands again?" Because by then the feel of the hands during the swing will be yours. Also, don't feel the need to tackle the whole book at once. You may get so much benefit, so much improvement from the Hands Chapter that you don't want to do any more for a while. Great! Davis certainly didn't feel the need to write away for the tango the day after he'd mastered the fox-trot. Golf is a lifelong pursuit. No need to make it a job. Every time you spend 10 or 15 minutes doing one of our exercises you are developing a little more feel. The gain in feel will not always be easy to measure. But eventually it will show up, not only in your score but in the way you hold the club, swing, even walk down the fairway.

## Teaching yourself

You may ask yourself why two fellows who have made their living teaching golf would create a book that ostensibly allows the reader to learn the swing by himself, why, indeed, they would feel it was even possible. It's our contention that while learning by oneself is harder than learning with a good teacher, it has been underestimated as a means of improving. We've seen too many golfers act as if a lesson every two months solves all their problems. All things being equal, you can do much more in your spare time than we can in a 50-minute lesson. That's how you learned to walk, to tie your shoes, to button a button. You can learn to swing a golf club that way, too.

At the same time, remember that images take hold when your mechanics are reasonably sound. There is a place for memorization, just as there was a place for those dance "maps" on Davis' floor. As you begin each chapter, study the illustrations of Bob swinging. Learn to identify the proper position of your club, your hands, your arms, etc., during the swing. Take tracing paper and trace the part of the club or body you're working on at the time. Give yourself quizzes. Where is the blade pointing at the top of the swing? Where is my right palm halfway through the backswing? Copy the positions in a mirror. Learn them so you can stop thinking about them when they become automatic.

## The swing principle

One last, very important point. Understanding the proper movement of the club—the shaft and the clubhead—is essential. Pick up a club. Hold it by the grip with your thumb and forefinger and let it swing. That's your golf swing in miniature. It is the golf club—not you—that strikes the ball. The more your body supports—and the less it interferes with—the swinging motion of the golf club, the more efficient and powerful a swing you will create. In their landmark report on the scientific principles of the golf swing, *The Search for the Perfect Swing,* Alastair Cochran and John Stobbs recount how one of the nongolfing members of their research team, who had analyzed the power of the swing on paper but had never seen a golfer in action, was convinced that the swing would be a "violent effort." "This so colored his expectation . . . that he was very startled indeed when he saw for the first time how smoothly and gently a professional seemed to be swinging at the ball, yet still producing the power he himself had predicted." Later the authors reveal the source of that nonviolent power: centrifugal force, "which (the golfer) uses to help him sling out, into the clubhead, the accumulated momentum of his body action. . . . This force rises to a peak of over a hundred pounds near the bottom of the swing for about a 10th of a second. . . ." Cochran and Stobbs and many other researchers have made believers out of us. Other researchers have determined that the greater the difference between the body weight of the person swinging an implement and the weight of the thing being swung, the less effective is leverage—hitting—and the more effective is centrifugal force—swinging. Speed and power in the swing, therefore, emanate not from the player's strength but from the centrifugal force of the clubhead itself.

Centrifugal defines the force that propels an object—in this case, the clubhead—outward from a center of rotation. Remember the girl on the swing? She is propelled outward from the point where the swing chains meet the crossbar. It also describes the force that the object exerts on the medium—the chains of the swing or the shaft of the club. Your job, like the girl's, is to surrender to the swing.

The more you allow that to happen, the farther and straighter you'll hit the ball. That's why, in the teaching world, we're "swingers." Some teachers think you can master positions and those positions, once mastered, will create the swing. But without the soul that is centrifugal force, those positions are useless, for your swing has no "swing." The message of this book is, "Propel the ball with the clubhead—and stop trying to hit it with your body."

If you have been a hitter or pounder or slugger of the golf ball, surrender to the sense of swing. Make that your goal, even if you feel at first that you're losing power. With every exercise, with every ball you hit, with every round you play, get a better feel of that clubhead swinging. Remember the girl on the swing. Or recall the image used by the great instructor Ernest Jones who swung a pen knife back and forth at the end of a long kerchief to teach that swinging motion. Keep a picture like that in your mind.

## Your Game Plan

At the end of each chapter you will find a game plan. It will help you master the movements of the body part you are working on. Take time to follow each of the steps that are part of every game plan:

A) Study the positions in the swing-sequence drawings and place yourself and your club in each of them, checking to see that your positions match the drawings.

B) Test yourself. Swing into each position without looking; guess if the position is correct; look and correct if necessary; then look away and get the feel. Repeat until you are successful the first time.

C) Swing through the positions in slow motion, recapturing the feel.

D) Hit balls while swinging in slow motion.

E) When you're making solid contact, hit balls with normal swings.

Note: Steps B and D are critical. Don't skip over them. Those are the drills that will develop your feel quickest. Step B teaches you to make decisions by feel. In Step D you expand that sense of feel from one of feeling positions to feeling motion. Those skills are what allow you to play by feel. We've talked to and taught many great players. Inevitably, they reveal that this is how they taught themselves to swing.

There are more related drills and exercises that will allow you to start feeling a great golf swing.

# 2 FEELING THE ENTIRE CLUB

Feeling the club is the key to feeling your swing. It's the clubhead that sends the ball to the target. And it's your sensation of the clubhead and the shaft during the swing that allows you to make it a well-timed and accurate one.

Because it happens so fast, it's difficult to see how the entire club moves. But understanding the movement is essential to letting it happen, or correcting it when it fails to. By studying the positions of the clubhead and shaft in these sequential drawings, you will learn the proper swinging motion of the club. Learn these positions now and you'll be able, when things go wrong, to recreate them and recapture the correct feel. Like Davis' dance-step diagrams from Arthur Murray, which told him exactly where his body should be touching the dance floor, this chapter will tell you how the club must swing in order to contact the ball squarely.

## How the face moves

Do you know, or can you feel, what someone means when he says your clubface is open or shut at the top of your swing? Or at impact? Being able to check for yourself is critical to becoming a "feel" player. When you've completed this chapter you'll know—and feel—what those positions are.

Let's first look at the clubface. An easy way to understand the changing positions of the clubface during the swing is to relate them to the directions of a compass. Let's

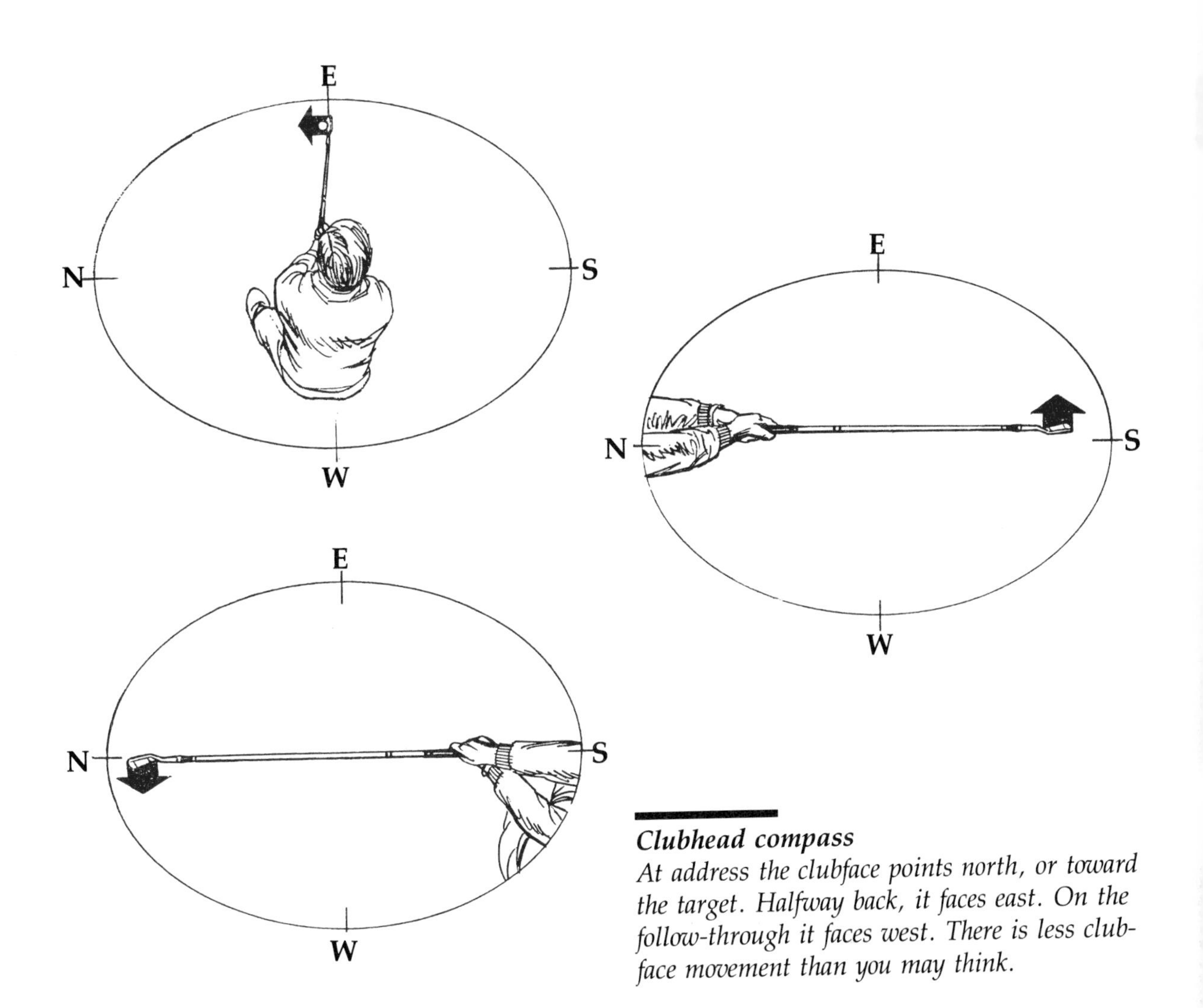


***Clubhead compass***
*At address the clubface points north, or toward the target. Halfway back, it faces east. On the follow-through it faces west. There is less clubface movement than you may think.*

say that the target line—the line pointing from your ball to the target—is facing north (see illustration). So the clubface, at address, is also facing north. Halfway through the backswing, the clubface faces east, or 90 degrees from where it started. From its position halfway through the backswing to the top of the backswing, its direction is still mostly eastward. Halfway through the downswing the clubface still faces eastward. Then, from that point to impact, it changes direction again and is pointing "northward" when it meets the ball. Halfway through the follow-through it is pointing westward. And at the end of the follow-through the face is still pointing westward.

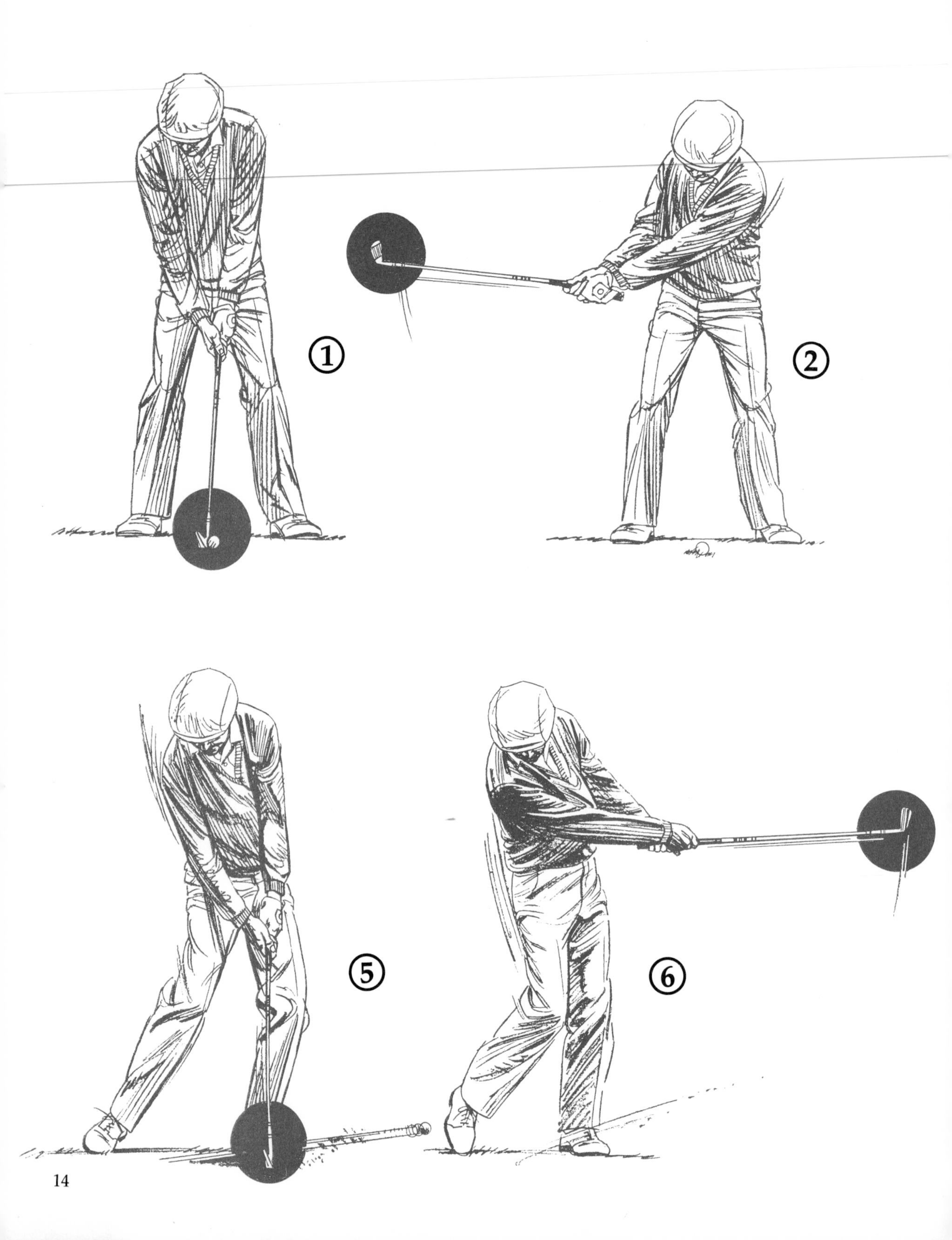
①
②
⑤
⑥

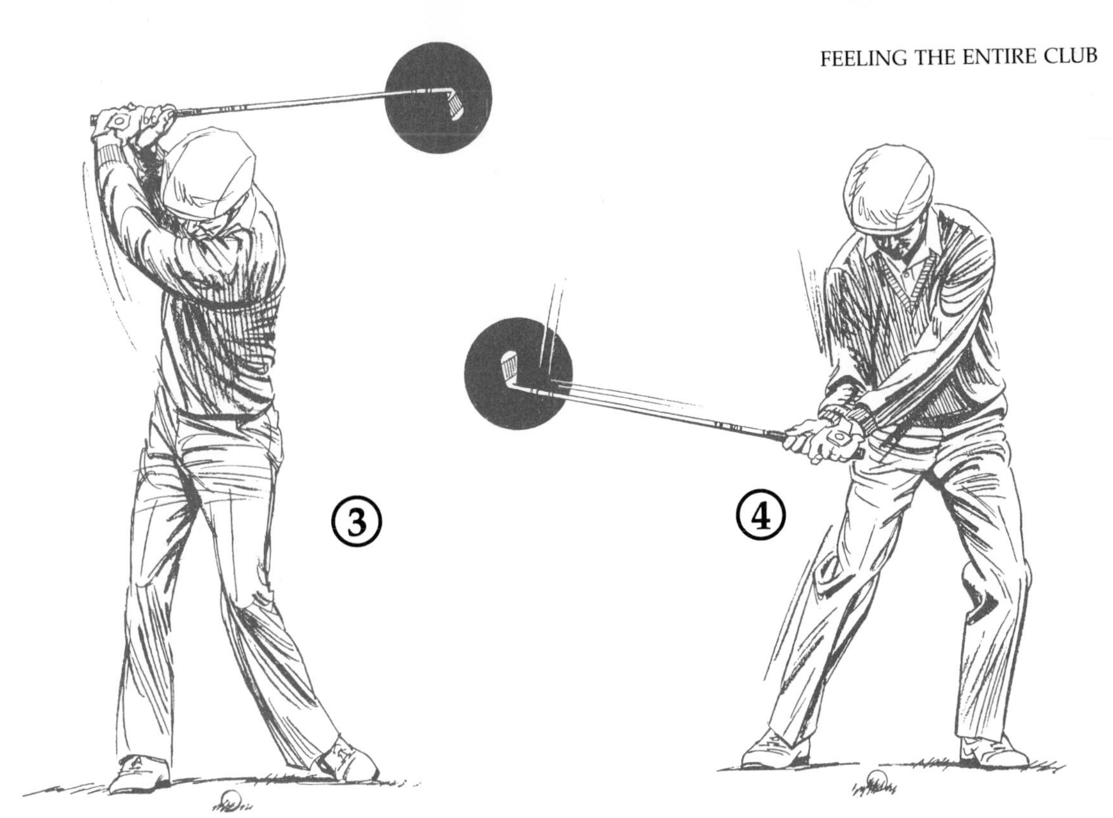

# The Clubhead

## Knowing its movement is the first step toward feeling your golf swing.

## Open, closed and square

You've heard people talk about the face of the club being "open" or "closed" at the top of the backswing. What do they mean? A closed clubface faces skyward at the top of the backswing. An open clubface faces dead east. With a 5-iron, the correct "square" position has the clubface looking at the sky at about a 45 degree angle.

**What's "square"?**
*A square 5-iron clubface faces the sky at about a 45 degree angle at the top of the swing. A closed face looks more toward the sky, an open face, less.*

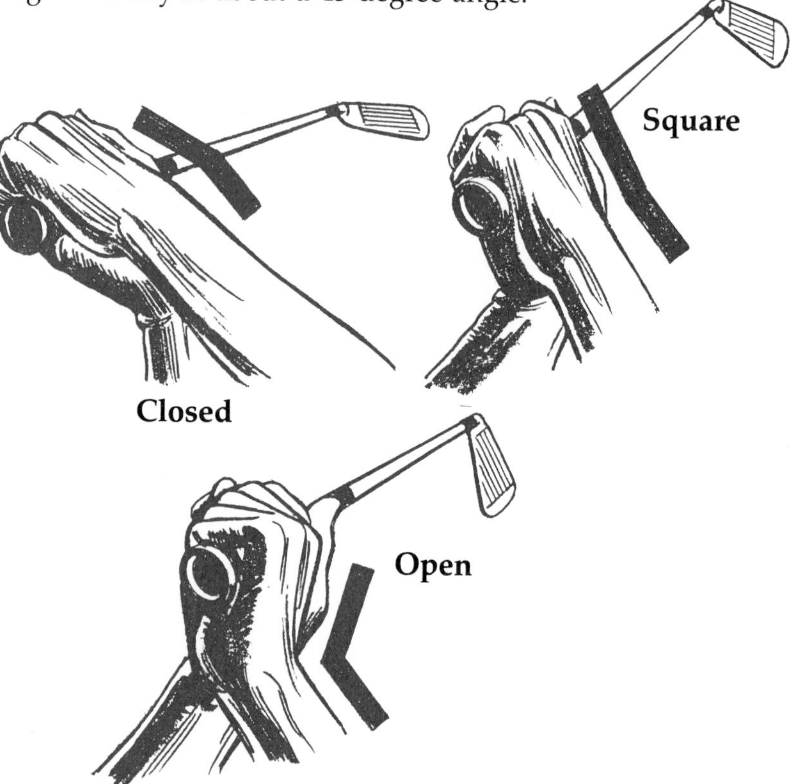


## Minimum of movement

To a few of you it comes as a surprise that there is as much as 90 degrees rotation in the direction of the clubface during the pre-impact part of the swing. But I'm willing to bet that most of you are surprised that there is so little rotation. We hope it will simplify your notion of the swing to know that the clubface changes direction as little as it does, and that it starts changing early in the backswing. To those of you who take the club back as if you wanted to hold the clubface in the address position (northward), however, this will seem like a lot of movement. But the clubface must change direction to allow the shaft to swing.

Another way to describe the movement of the clubface is that it opens like a door on a hinge, in this case the "hinge" is the shaft. By the time the clubhead reaches the halfway point in the backswing, the "door" is open 90 degrees. Although different players take more or less time to open that "door," almost all have opened it 90 degrees by the time the shaft of the club is halfway through the backswing, parallel to and pointing directly away from the target. From the player's point of view, most of the movement of the clubhead to this point has been in front of him.

## Shaft movement

All rotation of the shaft occurs from the beginning to the halfway point of the backswing, where the shaft reaches a line parallel to the ground. On the downswing, rotation occurs from the point where the shaft is again parallel to the ground to the same position on the follow-through. There is no turning of the shaft from the time it is halfway through the backswing (Position 2 in the sequential drawings) to the time it is halfway through the downswing (Position 4). The shaft swings around and up until it lies on what you might call an imaginary "clothesline" running behind the player's head, parallel to the target and parallel to the ground. But it does not rotate.

If, at the top of the backswing, the shaft points left of the target, it is said to be "laid off." If it points right of the target it is said to be "crossed over." Both positions are off the imaginary clothesline. These incorrect positions force the player to make compensations on the downswing to return the club to square.

The movement of the club is a natural movement. The club creates its own path based on its length and lie (the angle at which it rests on the ground). Our job is to train our bodies to swing the club along that path.

Eventually, you won't have to check whether your position is correct. You'll feel it. But take time now to memorize the proper positions of the shaft and clubface at various points during the swing. Identify a square-face position at the top of the swing, then close it, or open it and see what that feels like. Be able to identify laid-off, crossed-over or on-line shaft position. Watch the golfers you play with and try to identify face and shaft positions—good and bad—at different points in their swings.

When you know these positions, you can correct yourself. If you think your clubface is closed, for example, you can swing to the top and have a friend hold the shaft in position while you walk around and check.

## Your Game Plan

1. Study the illustrations of the clubhead swinging on pages 14-15.

2. Get the feel of open-, closed- and square-clubface positions halfway through the backswing, at the top, halfway down and at impact. Follow steps A, B and C on p. 11 until you've got them totally by feel.

3. Get the feel of the movement of the shaft during the swing. Follow steps A, B and C until you've got it.

4. Place the club along the "clothesline" at the top of the swing; then "lay it off," next "cross it over." Swing into the correct position until you have it by feel.

5. Make mini-swings (from hip to hip), ingraining the opening and closing of the face in the first part of the backswing and follow-through.

6. On the range, watch other players. Try to identify the face and shaft positions—good and bad—of their clubs halfway back, at the top and at impact.

▽ ▽ ▽ ▽ ▽ ▽ ▽ ▽ ▽ ▽

# 3
# FEELING YOUR HANDS

"Some players might as well stick their hands in their pockets," said the great golf instructor Seymour Dunn, "for all the use they make of them." Think back to the swing in the park. Let's say it's not a swing now, but a tennis ball hanging from a rope attached to the swing crossbar. You find it at rest and you want to start it swinging. How do you begin? Do you butt it with your body or nudge it with your shoulder? Do you push the rope with your arm? Or do you set it gently swinging with an easy push of your hand so that the ball climbs and falls back before you send it on its way again? And if you use your hand, do you clench it tightly or hold it just firmly enough to start it on the natural path limited by the length of the rope? Do you stiffen your wrist or let it flex? Which will keep the ball moving without bowing or jerking the rope? In a similar way, do you "flick" your wrist slightly at the bottom of the club's arc to add speed and send it forward faster? Or do you twist your body and lunge forward to quicken the club's pace?

The freedom and motion that we spoke of in Chapter 1 emanate from the hands. The hands start the clubhead moving, keep it on its natural path and sustain its centrifugal motion. It would take very little movement on your part to get that tennis ball moving at its maximum speed, and most of the movement would come from your hands. And so with your golf swing.

The hands, Dunn said, are the leaders of the swing. And

that surprises most golfers. You see them on the practice range struggling to lift the club with their arms or pull it with their shoulders or help it along with their legs and trunk. They twist and turn and slap and hit, clutching the club in a grip so tight their hands lose all of their natural power. "Most poor golfers," Ernest Jones said, "merely use their hands to hold the club. They don't understand that it is through the hands and fingers alone that they can influence the behavior of the club."

If that shoe fits you, here's some good news: The golf swing is easier than you thought, much easier when you master the movement of the hands. If you read no other chapter in the book, but work on the drills and exercises in this chapter, your game would—will—improve markedly. First, because your hands generate clubhead speed. Second, because your hands impose the greatest influence on the face of the club. Third, because your hands lead your arms in creating clubhead path. And finally, because they control the amount of tension in your swing. (If your hands are tight, your forearms become tight, your shoulders become tight, and so on.) In short, your hands are the boss. They control the speed at which you can swing and therefore the distance you can hit the ball. They control the accuracy with which you hit it.

***The leaders***
*Most golfers merely use their hands to hold the club. Actually, the hands control your swing.*

To begin to master these controllers of the swing, study the accompanying illustrations of Bob's swing. Note the position of his hands at address, halfway through the backswing, at the top of the backswing, halfway through the downswing, at impact and in the follow-through. Study how his hands grip the club.

In a minute we will examine the grip in detail and ask you to copy the positions of the hands during the swing. But first, recapture the feeling of the swing itself by taking the grip end of a club by the thumb and forefinger as you did in Chapter 1 and letting the club swing. Notice how much movement you can create by merely holding the club, with hardly any movement of your fingers. Or, following Ernest Jones' example, swing a pen knife at the end of a kerchief. As you develop your grip and learn the movements of the hands during the swing, try to duplicate that free-swinging motion. Your hands' job is to allow the club to swing. If you ever feel lost in the course of working on your swing, go back to these simple exercises. And, through your hands, let the club swing.

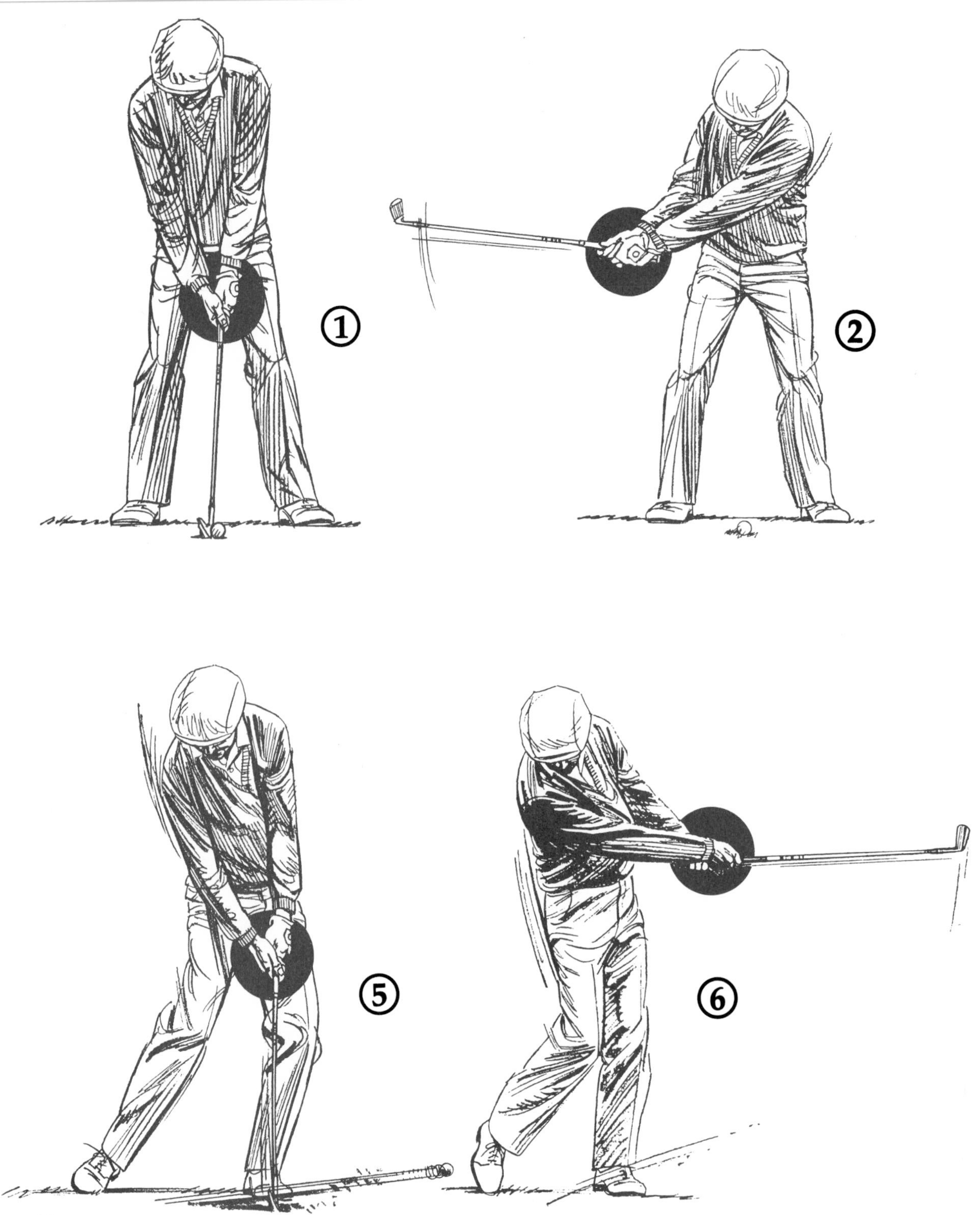
①
②
⑤
⑥

# Your Hands

They generate clubhead speed. They control the face. They shape the path of your swing.

***Jones' penknife***
*Ernest Jones had his students swing a kerchief and penknife to feel their hands creating the swinging motion. Try it. Keep the kerchief taut.*

## The feel of your grip

Some teachers speak about "weak" or "strong" grips. Grips aren't really weak or strong. They either allow the club to swing properly or they don't. We'll help you develop a neutral grip, one that will allow the swing to occur with no unnecessary compensations or reactions by your arms and body. That means a grip in which the left and right hands are equal partners. To help you establish that grip, let's do an exercise. We call it the Yardstick Drill and for those of you who have placed the club either too much in the palms or too much in the fingers of your hands, it will be a lifesaver.

It's very simple. Take two yardsticks (or one, cut in half) and fasten the two pieces against one another (see illustration). Now lay the yardsticks flat across your left hand with the bottom edges running along the calluses at the base of your fingers. Curl your fingers around the yardsticks, noticing that they slide up into your palm slightly as you do. Now "fit" your right hand to your left and place the yardsticks in your address position. There's your grip.

Study it. Absorb the feeling of it. Play with it. Turn your hands and see how the movement changes the "clubface" at the other end of the yardsticks. Feel your hands work together as you change positions.

Another exercise: With the yardsticks pointed away from you, cock your wrists up and down. The movement should be free and uninhibited. If you have been gripping your club too much in your palms—as many golfers do—the wrist cock is much greater than it has been (see illustration).

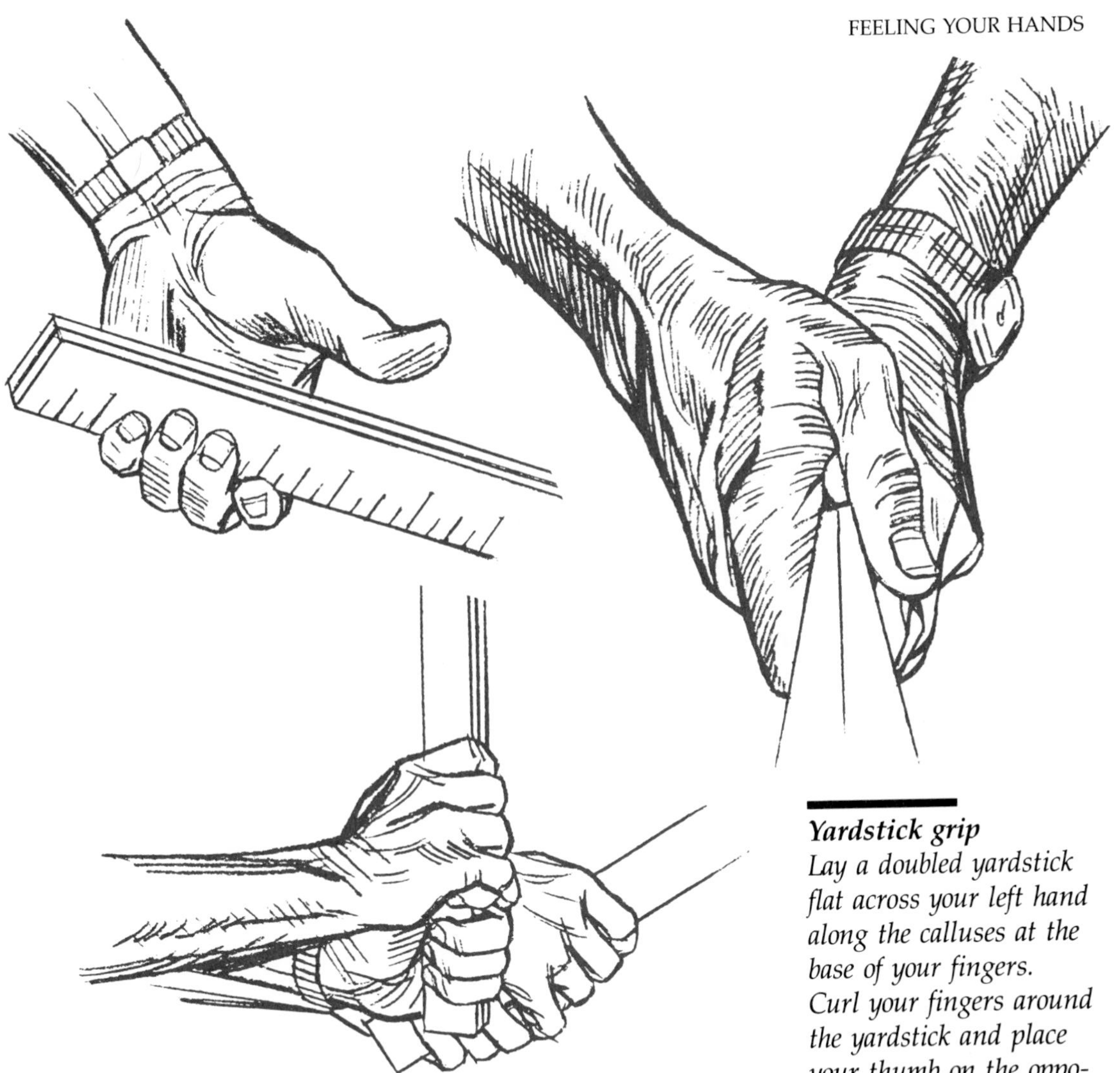

**_Yardstick grip_**
*Lay a doubled yardstick flat across your left hand along the calluses at the base of your fingers. Curl your fingers around the yardstick and place your thumb on the opposite side. Now fit your right hand to your left. Check the freedom your grip allows by cocking and recocking your wrists with the yardstick pointed away from you (bottom).*

Chances are this grip—now and when you transfer it to a club—feels somewhat "weaker" than your old grip. The fact is, while it may feel weaker at address, it will feel much stronger at impact.

Now let's transfer your yardstick grip to a golf club. Place your left hand on the club so it duplicates the feel of your left hand on the yardsticks. Before you put your right hand on, turn your left hand palm up, still holding the club. The handle of the club ought to lay diagonally across your left hand from the first knuckle of your index finger to just under the pad of your palm. Here is a quick check on the position of the club in your left palm. Take your left hand grip. With the club nestled under the heel pad, curl only your index finger around the shaft. Now try to swing the

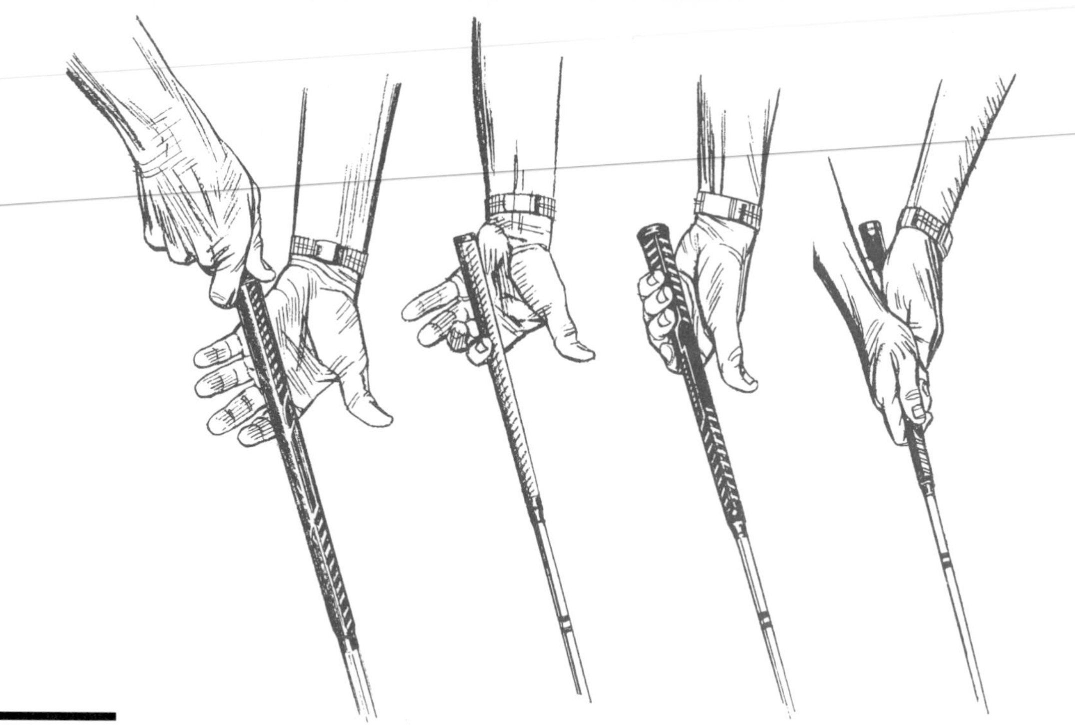

***Gripping the club***
*Lay the grip across your left palm, just under the pad, as you did the yardstick. Check the position by lifting the club while holding on with only your index finger. Then curl the fingers of your left hand around the grip and fit your right to your left.*

club gently in front of you. If the butt end of the club is correctly placed under the pad of your hand, it will stay in place (see illustration). If not, it will slip and slide and fall out of your hand.

Now curl the last three fingers of your left hand around the club. Place your thumb along the right side of the grip. Make sure it's extended down the shaft far enough to allow the fleshy base of the thumb to lie against the fingertips. Be sure also to retain the holding strength of the last three fingers of your hand. You left hand is set. As you look down at your left-hand grip in the direction of the ball, it's normal to see the first two knuckles of your hand.

Now the right hand: First, fit the "lifeline" of the right palm onto the left thumb. Second, curl your fingers around the grip. Third, check your right hand position to see if the line formed by your right thumb and forefinger point to your chin. It should. Make sure the thumb and forefinger are not touching. The right thumb lies along the left side of the grip.

This grip allows you to control the club with your fingers while letting your hands and forearms work together. If the shaft lies too much in your fingers, your forearms and hands work separately and you lose control and power. Think of a boxer. If he punches you with his fingers curled into themselves, he has no punch. If he presses his fingers against his palm, the blow is also a weak one. But if he curls them into his palm, look out. You want a grip that maximizes power, that allows the speed you create with your hands to be transmitted without wasted effort into your arms. If the grip is too much in your fingers, you lose swing speed. If it is too much in your palm, you lose flexibility. The "yardstick" grip gives you the best of both worlds.

Taking your grip is the job of your hands. It should not involve your shoulders. To check this, take your left hand off the club and start all over. This time place your left hand on the club while your left arm is hanging at your side. (Again, recreate the feeling you had with the yardsticks.) Bring the club out in front of you and put it in address position. Now, without involving your right shoulder, bring your right hand around and fit it to the left. Go through this procedure over and over again until you can recreate the "yardstick" grip totally by feel.

***Shoulder check***
*Taking your grip is your hands' job, not your shoulders'. Bring your right hand to your left without involving your right shoulder (as Davis demonstrates on the left). Using your shoulder (right) causes the right forearm to get above the left, complicating your swing.*

Here's how to test your "quiet" right shoulder. Stand facing one side of a door frame (see illustration). Now slap your right hand against the wall on the right side of the frame. But slap it so that the movement begins with your hand and does not involve your right shoulder. Continue until you have the sensation of the hand leading, the arm following and the shoulder remaining "soft." Note how that placement of the right hand against the frame resembles the movement of the right hand and arm during the downswing.

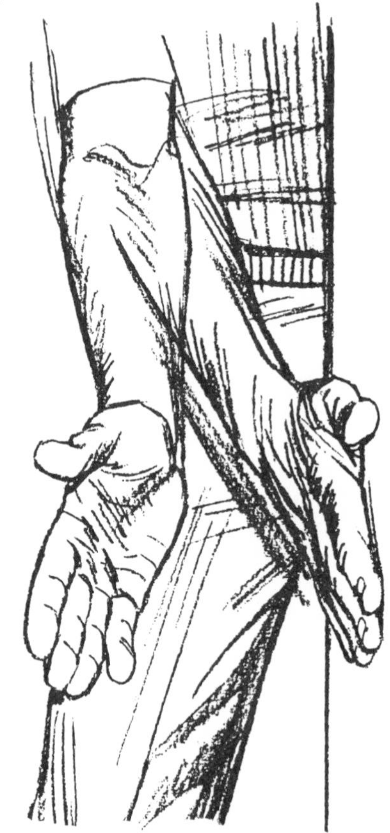

***Frame test***
*Test the "quietness" of your right shoulder by facing a door frame and bringing your right hand around to slap the wall. If your shoulder gets involved, your hand won't land flush on the wall.*

Take your grip once more with a 5-iron, starting with the left hand at your side. When both hands are on the club, hold it up in front of you so that the shaft is horizontal. Feel the connection between your hands and the clubhead, especially the relationship between the back of your left hand and the face of the club (see illustration). You might want to move your hands down the shaft so that they are closer to the face of the club. Turn your hands and watch the clubhead turn.

With your hands back on the grip, let the club swing back and forth from waist high on the backswing to waist high on the follow-through. Watch the clubface and feel your hands. Now close your eyes and guess the position of the clubhead, based only on the feel in your hands. Eventually you will learn to do this as you hit balls.

A final note on your grip. Some teachers talk about having a "long" or "short" left thumb, referring to the distance the thumb extends down the shaft. We don't think you have a choice. The thumb must be "long" enough to give maximum gripping control with the last three fingers of your left hand without reducing wrist flexibility. If the thumb is too long or too short the fingers will be pulled out of place. In either case, you lose control of the club at the top of your backswing. You know players whose hands almost come off the club at the top of their swings. Often the reason is that they did not establish a firm enough hold with those last three fingers, the result of a left thumb that was too long or too short.

***Left hand is key***
*Monitor the position of the clubface by feeling the position of your left hand. These two positions should be close to parallel throughout the swing.*

We recommend that you grip the club as though you were gluing your hands to it. Or as though your hands and the grip were Velcro. You want complete contact. Every bit of the insides of your fingers should be touching the rubber grip. No gaps. No air pockets. No spaces.

Having the correct grip size makes that easy. The size of your golf grips should correspond to the size of your hands. When you close the fingers of your left hand around the grip, the tip of your middle finger should just barely be touching the palm of your hand. You'll have an easier time gripping the club with your right hand if the grip "taper" is right for you; that is, if the diameter of the grip decreases toward the clubhead to allow the club to fit naturally into the fingers of your right hand. If the grip is too thick at the point where your right thumb and index finger hold the club, it will tend to ride out of the fingers and into the palm. That weakens your right hand, making it harder for you to bring the club back to square at impact. Manufacturers once tapered grips more than they do today. Some still do. Those grips are worth hunting for.

## Grip pressure: How tight?

Nothing can sabotage a good grip or a good swing quicker than excessive or inconsistent grip pressure. Tension is the enemy of the swing and it emanates from the grip. If your fingers are tense, your forearms become tense. That tension spreads to your upper arms, your shoulders and your back. Believe it or not, excessive grip pressure can make it all but impossible to turn and rotate your body correctly. What's more, you can't feel a thing when you're gripping the club too tightly so your short game is shot, too. In sum, tension is a destroyer—of freedom, of rhythm, of motion itself.

Whenever you have doubts about grip pressure, test it. As you hit practice shots, establish a pressure at address of four or five on a scale of 10. At the finish of your swing, call out the new level: six, 10, whatever it is. Don't do anything about it. Just call it out. Start each shot at four or five and keep calling out the new pressure level at the finish of your swing. We'll bet it's higher at the finish than at the start. But you'll discover simply by being aware of it that that second level will come down and more closely conform to the first. Your goal here is a grip pressure that remains relatively constant through the swing. How tight should it be? Pick up a pencil and write your name. How tightly did you hold the pencil? Just tightly enough to accomplish the task at hand. Which is how you hold your steering wheel, how you hold a book, how you hold your sweetheart's hand. For most golfers, holding a golf club only as tightly as enables the club to swing will seem much lighter than normal.

## Feeling hands and wrists together

Hands and wrists work together in the swing, but not as though they are welded or locked in place. A lot of golfers seem to think they can simplify the full swing by locking hands and wrists into a single unit. That only complicates matters. Get a hammer, a nail and a small piece of wood. Really do it. After you have the nail started place the wood so that the surface is vertical. Now tap in the nail. It's wrist flexibility that gives you the "snap" to drive the nail in. Try pounding the nail with your wrist stiff. You might think driving the nail would be easier to control that way, but it's much harder. You have no power and you can't find the nail.

It's the same when you hit a golf ball. The motion of a chip shot is like that of tapping a nail with a small hammer. As you make bigger swings your motion changes but the hand-wrist relationship is still critical. With a large hammer, or your golf club, you add rotation and lateral movement, but at the striking point the hand-and-wrist action is almost the same.

Here's a drill to increase your hand-wrist dexterity. Hold

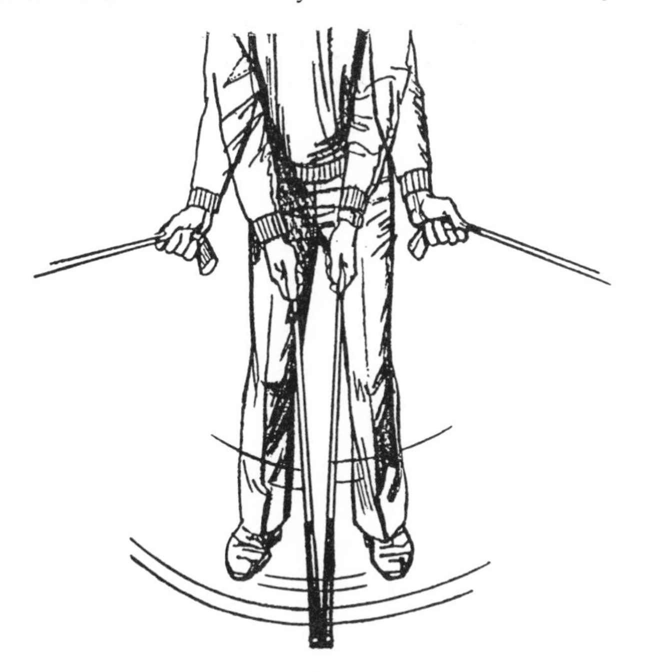

***Tap Drill***
*Holding an iron in each hand by the clubhead, tap the grips together as many times as you can. Notice how grip pressure affects your ability to make the ends meet.*

one iron club by the clubhead in each hand. Point the grips toward the floor and tap them together (see previous illustration). Not as easy as it looks, is it? Tap them together until you make dozens of taps in succession. Notice that it becomes easier as you "soften" your hands and let the feel of the movement take over. When you are doing the drill well, observe your grip pressure and the flexibility in your wrists. Stiffness and pressure may at first feel like control—but they only make the task tougher.

## Hand positions during the swing

Your grip is set. You know the importance of proper grip pressure and flexible wrists. Now let's swing. Turn to the sequential illustrations. Grab a 6- or 7-iron and find a mirror or window in which you can see yourself make some movements. Like Davis with his dance diagrams, your first job is to familiarize yourself with the positions, then to swing through them slowly and finally to feel them in the full swing. Motion without proper positioning won't work. But neither will correct positioning without fluid motion. Your feel will marry the two.

Most of this you can do indoors. Eventually you'll need a little more room. But, please, don't lay this book down, rush out to the range and start hitting balls. There's no hurry.

## Address

Start with address. Grip the club. Close your eyes. Absorb the feel of the grip and your hand positions. Now start all over and this time don't open your eyes until you think you've matched Bob's grip and hand position in the illustration. Your grip is right. Your clubhead is square to your "target line." Check it.

Go through the same procedure with the position halfway through the backswing. Set yourself. Close your eyes and get the feel of it. Place yourself in the position without looking. Check it. Do the same with the hand positions at the top of the backswing, halfway through the downswing, at impact, halfway through the follow-through and at the finish. Do each over and over again until you can feel the correct hand positions in your sleep. Don't worry for now about whether your arms or legs or body look right. Your only concern is your hands.

## Swinging back

In a moment we'll connect those hand positions in a slow-motion swing. But first let's do a drill that will give you the feel of the correct motion going back. It's called the Hitchhike Drill and it's one of the most effective we know. Put your club down for a moment, place your right hand behind your back and take an imaginary address position with

***Hitchhike drill***
*To get a feel for proper hand motion during the swing, place your right arm behind you and swing your left arm so that your left thumb touches your right shoulder on the backswing and your left shoulder on the follow-through. Do it over and over until your motion is rhythmic and natural.*

your left. Now, while making a full turn, swing your left thumb back until it touches your right shoulder (see illustration). Then swing it through until it touches your left shoulder on the follow-through. Keep going back and forth until you are making a natural, rhythmic swing. Now hold a club with your left hand only and swing to the top, keying on your left thumb. Notice that at address your thumb points down. Halfway through the backswing it points directly away from the target. At the top it has turned straight up and over your right shoulder until is pointing toward the target (see illustration). Your club now is resting directly on your left thumb (a good, mid-swing checkpoint). On the downswing the thumb will reverse itself until, on the follow-through, it will point away from the target and over your left shoulder. Whenever you've lost the feel of your hand positions, especially on the backswing, return to the Hitchhike Drill.

***Thumb check***
*Make the "hitchhike" motion with a club in your left hand. On the takeaway, the thumb rests on top of the shaft and points away from the target. At the top, it's directly under the shaft.*

## Swinging down

As the Hitchhike Drill illustrates, the hand positions of the forward swing are almost a mirror image of those on the backswing. Let's now connect those hand positions in a slow-motion swing. Taking your normal grip and address position, swing the club through the positions a few times with your eyes closed, stopping randomly to check your hand positions against the illustrated ones. Once you've got the feel, make full, slow-motion swings with your eyes open. Notice how your hands and wrists work together, how the wrists follow the hands and cock and recock in response to your hands.

Finally, on the range, hit 9-iron or wedge shots, making one practice swing for every ball you hit. Don't worry about where the ball is going. Instead, concentrate on your hands. Let your sense of feel guide them into the right positions. Don't "place" them there. If you feel the need to do that, go back to the no-ball exercises and then to slow-motion swings to be sure you're swinging through the correct positions.

A note: Whenever you hit balls, hit some shots in slow motion, a method many world-class athletes use to refine technique. Sprinter Carl Lewis still runs at half speed to analyze and improve his near-perfect style. In golf, slow motion may be your key to greater power. When he was a teenager, Davis' son, Davis Love III, asked his father how to hit the ball longer. Davis suggested his son make full-length, slow-motion swings using a driver, while not allowing the ball to travel more than 50 yards. When young Davis could hit those 50-yard drives solid and straight, he graduated to 100-yard drives—still in slow motion. In 50-yard increments Davis III worked his way up to 300 yards. Today he can drive a ball 350 yards when he wants to and leads the PGA Tour in driving distance. Slow-motion swinging teaches you to "find" the ball with the clubface and to control the force of your swing. It teaches pace. Include some slow-motion swinging in every practice session.

## Impact

You'll note that we have not yet used the word "release" in this chapter on hand motion. In the golf swing, release means the rotation of the hands, wrists and forearms from their position on the backswing, back to a square position at impact, to their position on the follow-through. Some books spend a great deal of time talking about release. The fact is, if you study and master the hand movements in these diagrams with the drills we've given you, you shouldn't have to worry about release. Release will occur naturally when your hands and forearms are working in tandem.

Here's an exercise by master teacher Paul Runyan, the former PGA Champion, that promotes efficient hand, wrist and forearm coordination. It will also increase your hand and, therefore, clubhead speed. You can do it while you're watching TV. Stand up and put your left hand in front of you, palm facing toward you. Now flip the palm as fast as you can so that it faces away from your leg. Repeat it again and again, keeping your hand, wrist and forearm as loose and flexible as you can. Then do it with your right hand and arm, starting with the palm facing away from you and flipping back toward you. Now place both hands in their starting positions, move them together to your right and swing them back to your left, flipping the palms as quickly as you can as you go (see illustration). Repeat the movement over and over, starting slowly and increasing the speed of the "flip" of the wrists. Without touching a club, you've learned the correct movement of hands, wrist and forearms during the swing. You've also learned that the "softer" your hands, the faster they flip. Which begins to explain why tight grip pressure decreases, not increases, clubhead speed. Stiff hands and wrists are slow hands and wrists.

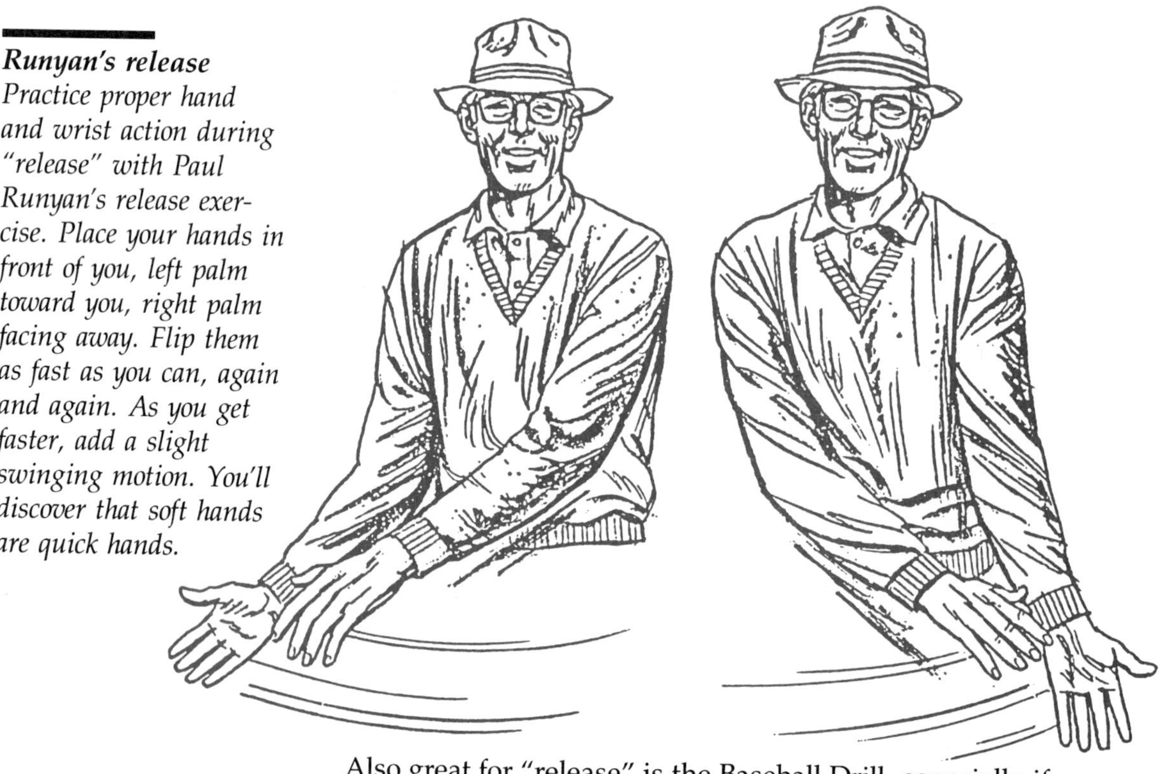

***Runyan's release***
*Practice proper hand and wrist action during "release" with Paul Runyan's release exercise. Place your hands in front of you, left palm toward you, right palm facing away. Flip them as fast as you can, again and again. As you get faster, add a slight swinging motion. You'll discover that soft hands are quick hands.*

Also great for "release" is the Baseball Drill, especially if you tend to slice the ball. Grip your club normally and begin to swing it at waist level the way you would a baseball bat. Gradually bend forward and lower the club to ground level, still thinking of a "level" swing. We've seldom seen a player who could slice the ball while trying to swing level.

If you went no farther in this book than this chapter on hands, and did no other exercises than these, we can almost guarantee that your handicap will drop several points. Take your time. Master this chapter's principles and exercises. When you're ready, go on to the next chapter.

## Your Game Plan

### □□Feeling the Clubhead

1. Hold a club between your thumb and forefinger and let it swing. Feel the weight of the clubhead, notice how it slows down on the way up, picks up speed on the way down.

### □□Grip

**1. The Yardstick Drill.** Lay two pieces of yardstick, taped or glued together, across the calluses of your left hand. Then fit your right to your left. Do it repeatedly until the "yardstick" grip feels natural to you.

2. Using the yardsticks, get the feel of the hand positions on pages 22-23 by completing steps A, B and C on page 11.

3. Now transfer your grip to a club, getting the feel of the positions by completing steps A, B and C.

4. Test the quietness of your shoulder by standing in a doorway, facing the frame, and bringing your right hand up and placing it flat against the wall.

### □□Hand-Wrist Relationship

1. Hammer a small nail into a vertical surface, noting the movements of your hand and wrist.

**2. Grip-tap Exercise.** Holding two iron clubs by their heads, tap the grips together, attempting to make as many taps in succession as you can.

### □□Hand Movements during the Swing

**1. Hitchhike Drill.** With no club, make a full turn and swing your left hand back from an imaginary address position until it points at your right shoulder. Then swing it down and across your body until it points at your left shoulder. Do it again and again in a swing-like motion, observing the movement of your hand.

**2. Runyan "Release" Exercise.** Stand with your left hand in front of you, palm in. Turn the hand to a palm-out position. Switch hands, this time starting with the right hand palm out and flipping it over. Then swing your hands from your right side to your left, turning the palms as you go. Try to do it faster and faster, allowing your wrists to get looser and looser.

**3. Slow-motion Shots.** After connecting the hand positions in the sequential drawings by following steps A-C on page 11, hit balls while making slow-motion swings. When your shots are solid and consistent, graduate to full-motion swings.

**4. Grip-pressure Exercise.** First without a ball, and then with, make swings with an iron club using a grip pressure at address of four or five on a scale of 1 to 10. Call out your grip pressure at the finish of each swing. Observe whether the beginning and ending pressure levels get closer.

# 4 FEELING YOUR ARMS

"We must consider the shoulders to be disastrous leaders but wholly admirable followers of the swinging motion created by the hands and arms," wrote Seymour Dunn.

Your arms support your hands. They transport your hands. And, taking their lead from your hands, they create rhythm in your swing. Your arms control the pace of your swing, just as they set your pace when you walk. And none of this can happen without arm freedom. Try walking with your arms held straight at your sides and you'll understand why. Your walk has no rhythm. It's the same with your golf swing. Unfortunately, many golfers put themselves in a hole from the start by restricting and tensing their arms.

So the keynote of this chapter is freedom. Freedom from pressure, freedom from tension, freedom of movement. Think of a mother rocking a child in her arms. Think of the little girl on the swing. Think of the elephant's trunk, powerful but flexible, swinging as the elephant walks.

As you study the arm drawings and do the arm exercises in this chapter, recall these images. It's important to know correct arm position during the swing, but remember that correct positioning and the subsequent generation of power begin with freedom of movement.

The importance of arm freedom is easy to grasp if you consider arm function in other sports. A pitcher can't generate speed if his arms aren't free to swing away from his body. The great pitchers such as Warren Spahn, Bob

Gibson and Don Drysdale allowed those arms to hang relaxed as they looked in for the sign and kept them flexible throughout the pitching motion. Tension is the enemy of speed. Isiah Thomas, a perennial NBA all-star, can't bounce a basketball if his arms are tense and tight at his sides. He extends them and keeps them relaxed to respond to the bounce of the ball and the action of his hands. In golf, your arms allow your hands to create swing speed; relaxed arms mean faster hands.

***Free arm-swing***
*Your goal: an arm swing as free and rhythmic as a child on a swing.*

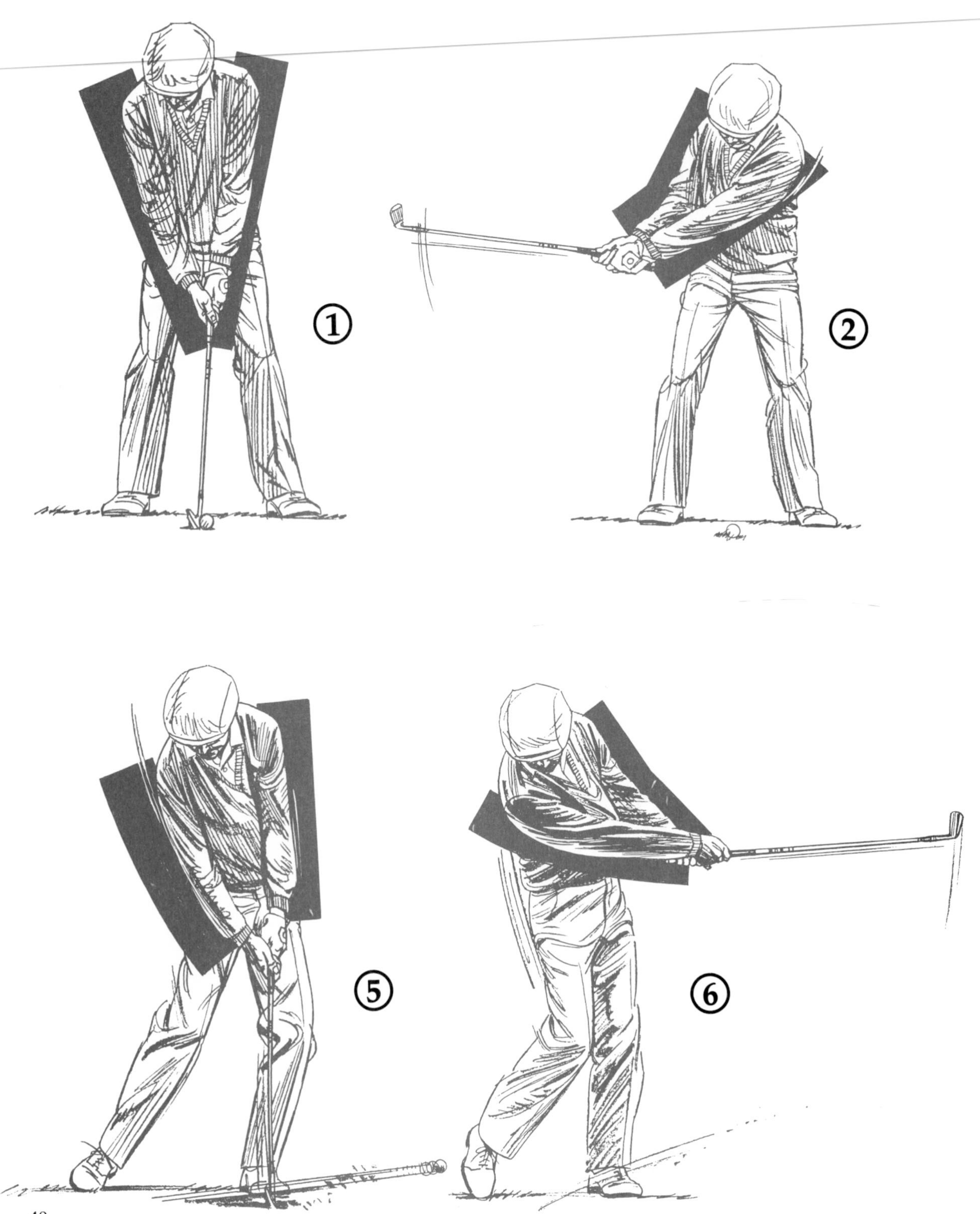
①
②
⑤
⑥

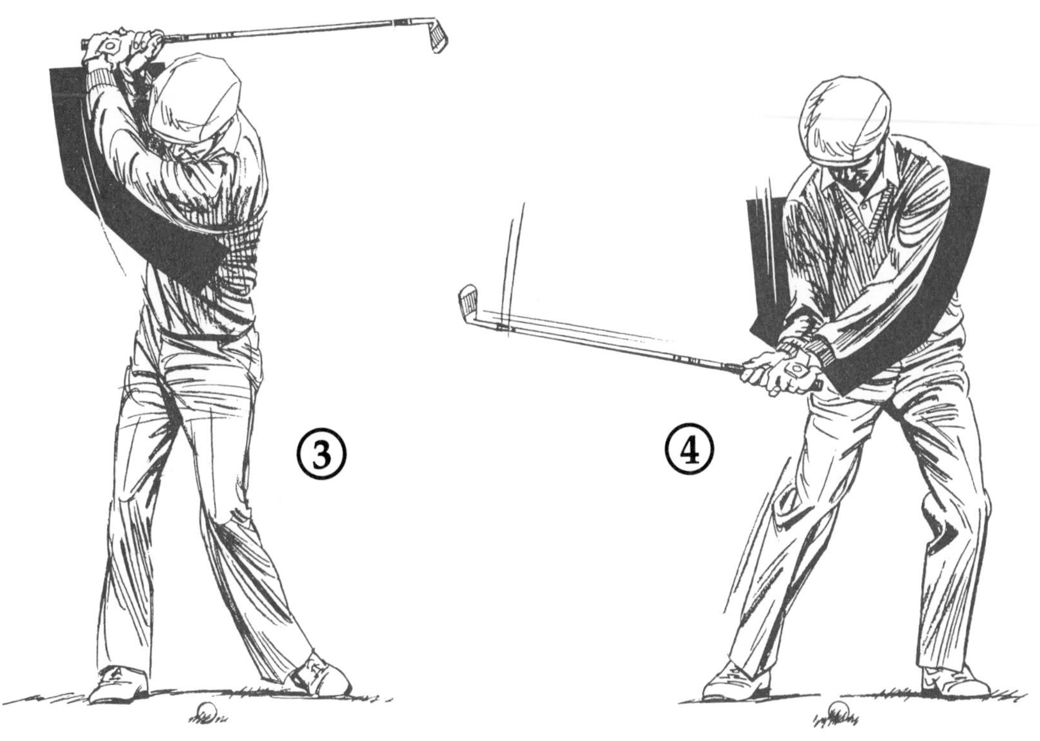

## Your Arms

Though they take their lead from your hands, your arms are the authors of rhythm and pace in your swing.

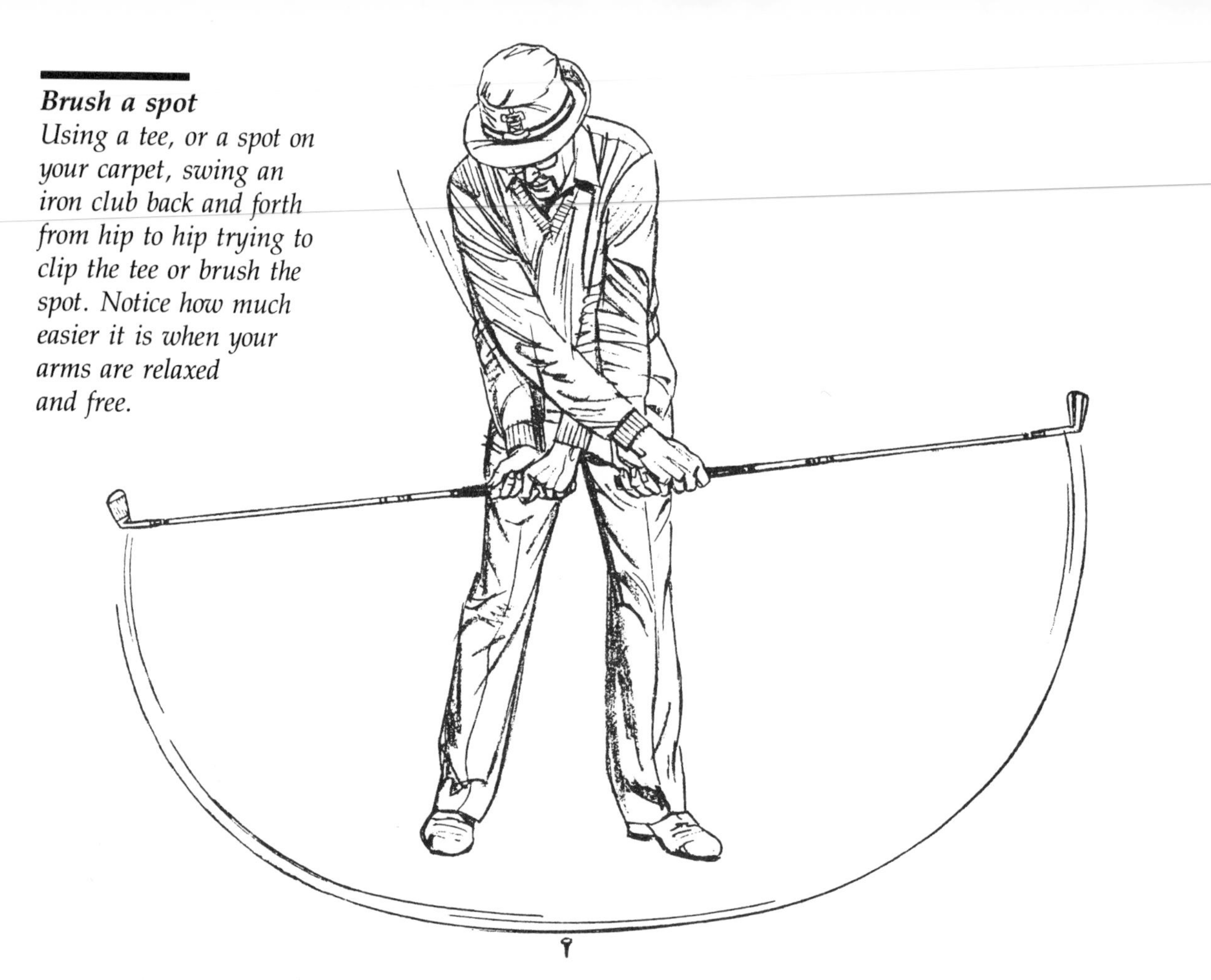

***Brush a spot***
*Using a tee, or a spot on your carpet, swing an iron club back and forth from hip to hip trying to clip the tee or brush the spot. Notice how much easier it is when your arms are relaxed and free.*

Here's an exercise to underscore the point. Pick a spot on the carpet (or put a tee in the ground outside) and swing an iron club back and forth at the spot, trying to brush the spot or clip the tee. You'll find that hitting the spot becomes easy and you can swish the club quite fast if your arms and hands are relaxed. Tighten them and suddenly it's very tough. Do it again and again until you can't miss the spot. "But that's obvious," you say. "C'mon, tell me where to put my arms. Tell me where they ought to be at address, at the top of my swing. Tell me how they ought to move." We will. But because so many golfers have lost that freedom of arm swing, let's address one more source of arm "slavery": the tyranny of the shoulders. You've probably noticed that there is no Shoulders Chapter in this book. Yet, if we were to write a book based on the way most golfers hit a golf ball, shoulders would be the first and longest chapter, in some cases the only chapter. Seymour Dunn recognized that many golfers' backswings begin with a jerk of the club away from the ball, instigated by the right shoulder, and that their downswings begin with a jerk of the club toward the ball, created by the left shoulder. These movements undermine the swing. Rather, the shoulders ought to be supporting your arms, which in turn support your hands.

It's our belief that the farther you go from your fingers and toes the more your movements are reaction rather than cause. Your shoulders, being far from your fingers, should not be treated as leaders but as followers. (The same goes for your hips.) Yet many golfers seem obsessed with "shoulder turn" (and hip turn). They work on their pivots, not realizing that how they pivot will be determined by how they swing their arms. If your arms swing the club vertically, for example, your shoulders will tilt or lift. If your arms swing the club around, your shoulders will turn. Therefore, begin this chapter by putting your shoulders in their place. As you study the arm positions and do the arm exercises, monitor the relationship between arms and shoulders. Which are leading which? By keeping your shoulders relaxed and "docile," you'll make it easier for your arms to create swing rhythm and for your hands to create swing speed.

## Creating arm motion

Pick up the kerchief and penknife you swung in the Hands Chapter. Let the penknife swing back and forth on the kerchief again. Now hold the kerchief with your left hand only and let your arm hang the way it would at address. Swing your left arm back and forth so that the penknife swings at the end of the kerchief. Notice what happens when your arm motion gets too fast or arrhythmic? Swing the kerchief until it is easy to keep it taut and to keep the penknife swinging. Please don't skip over this. It may seem silly or unimportant, but this little exercise will help you grasp the freedom of movement you'll need to master the arm swing. It will help you coordinate the movement of your hands and arms. And it will teach you why swinging the club at a pace that allows you to feel and follow the clubhead's own swing will give you more clubhead speed and control.

When swinging the kerchief and penknife is second nature, pick up a club and swing it while holding the kerchief against the grip, using the last three fingers of your left hand. Swing the club hip to hip (see illustration). Make small swings at first, then add length and speed, keeping the club and the kerchief swinging together. Next, swing

### *Club and kerchief*

*Get a feel for proper arm pace by swinging Ernest Jones' penknife and kerchief along with a club, holding the kerchief against the club with the last three fingers of your left hand. Keep the club and kerchief swinging together.*

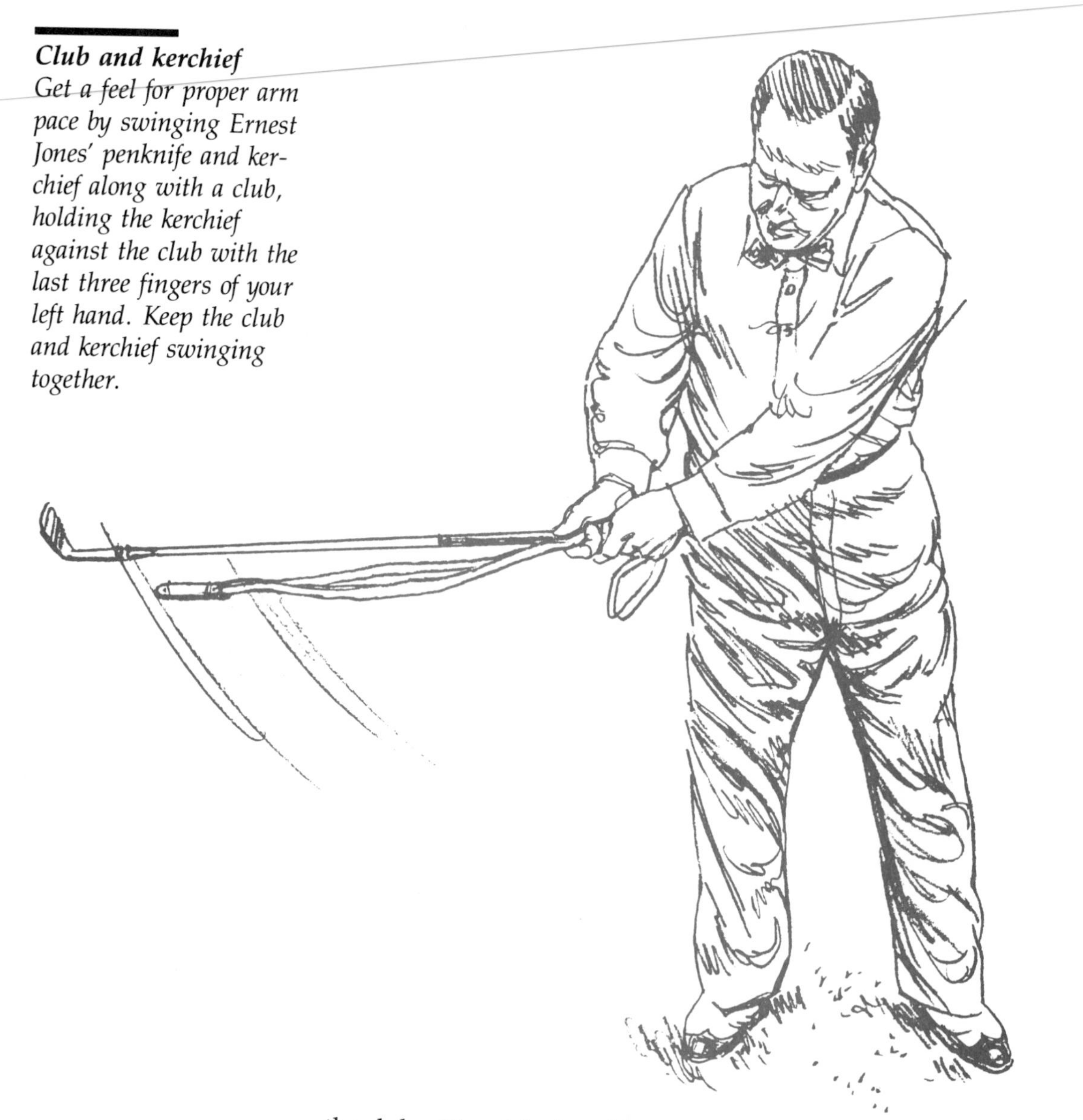

the club without the kerchief. Swing it faster and faster until the swing "breaks down." The last speed prior to your arm and the club getting out of sync is your optimum swing speed. If you're like most of our students, you're disappointed. "Gosh, do I have to swing that slowly?" The answer is, "Yes." Swinging faster than that will only increase arm tension and undermine a free swing, which will cost you the distance you probably hoped to gain by increasing your swing speed. Freedom, we repeat, is the key to both swing speed and power.

Here's an exercise to demonstrate how, once you've created that free arm motion, your body will follow it. Without a club, take your stance at address and align yourself to a specific target. Swing your arms back and forth toward the target as if you were going to hit the ball with your arms only. Get into it, make it easy and relaxed. Notice how your shoulders follow your arm swing and bring your torso into the swing. Suddenly, "shifting your weight" and "pivoting" aren't such a chore; you've let your hands and arms lead. Doing this exercise with a club in each hand will further emphasize the point (see illustration). It will also demonstrate how the pace of the arms either supports or undermines the natural sequence of hand, arm, body motion. Try it now. Holding an iron club in each hand make three-quarter swings, keeping your arms parallel to one another. As you work on other exercises in this chapter and copy the arm positions in the drawings, try to maintain the simplicity of this free arm swing.

***Two-clubs drill***
*To feel how your body takes its lead from your arms, make three-quarter swings with an iron in each hand. Swing easily enough so that the clubs move together.*

## Arm positions

Study the arm positions in the drawings. Take an iron club, put yourself in each arm position and then make a few slow, easy swings through those positions. Test yourself by placing your arms in the correct position at random points in the swing. After you've read through the commentary below and done the exercises, go back and retest yourself.

## Address

Arm freedom and simplicity of arm motion begin at address. Study the drawing of Bob's arms at address. Notice how the arms hang freely from the body. The upper arms are not squeezed against the chest as you see in some golfers. The left arm is extended but not rigid. The right arm is slightly bent and relaxed. Throughout the swing, the right arm will work around and about the left arm, just as the right hand works around and about the left hand. The left leads, the right supports.

The left arm is slightly higher than the right. The right elbow is folded. If you were to slide a club across the crook of the right elbow at address and point it at the target, the butt end would point directly at the middle of the left arm.

As you copy the address position, remember that your arms aren't steel rods. They have joints. We've noted that the right arm is bent, but so is the left if ever so slightly. Think of extending your left arm, not straightening it. The minute you try to straighten it, you lock your elbow joint. That will inhibit freedom of movement later, and it may cause you some pain. That straight left arm is why so many golfers suffer from "tennis elbow." Bob has cured his students of this by having them hit balls with their left arms bent throughout the swing. It's that left elbow socket that absorbs the shock of the club hitting the ball and the turf. So as you stand to address the ball, think of your arms as made of strong, resilient rubber—not steel.

An easy way to establish that flexibility is Paul Runyan's "Underreach" Drill. At address, suspend the club in the air behind the ball. Let the leading edge of the club hover just behind the equator of the ball. Now, without moving your head, allow your arms to lengthen so that the clubface sits squarely behind the ball. Then allow the blade to return to its "hovering" position. During the swing, allow that extension to happen naturally; the more relaxed your arms are, the easier it will be. By keeping their arms rigid most golfers prevent that extension and lose the clubhead speed it helps to create. Not surprisingly, one of the best and biggest hitters of all time, Jack Nicklaus, addresses every shot with the clubhead hovering off the ground.

## Swinging back

As the arms swing back, the left arm leads. It is the straighter of the two levers and it is the moving and supporting force of the swing. The trailing arm, the right arm, supports the left. (At impact it will do more than support, but even then the left arm must place the right arm in a position to deliver the clubhead to the ball.) The faster the right arm passes through the ball, the faster the left arm must move to support the right.

***Shake hands***
*On the takeaway, have the feeling that you are shaking hands with a person standing directly to your right. There is minimum of forearm rotation.*

Early in the backswing the forearms rotate. In the previous two chapters we discussed rotation of the clubshaft. We explained that the hands accomplish that rotation in the first half of the backswing. That movement causes the forearms to rotate. How much rotation is correct? Think of turning to shake hands with someone standing directly to your right. That's about how much rotation your forearms make by the time the shaft is parallel to the ground halfway through the backswing.

From that point, the job of the arms is to lift the club into an "on-line" position at the top of the swing, as described in Chapter 2. Their rotation should be complete by now. Now their job is transportation—transportation of the clubshaft to the correct position at the top, parallel to the ground and parallel to the target line. As we pointed out in the Hands Chapter, there is less work to do than most golfers think. There is no twisting or turning of the arms. They swing the club back, they lift it up, they set it over the shoulder.

What's more, there is plenty of time. Many golfers hurry on the backswing because they think that will make it easier for them to get the club on the proper path and to keep it there. Actually, that speed makes it more difficult to keep things in sync. Other golfers want to stop at the top to "place" the club in the proper position. That can be disastrous, too.

Try this to get the feel of proper pace: flip a coin. Watch it slow down as it reaches its apex. Not only does the coin travel more slowly, but it also makes fewer and fewer revolutions as it reaches the top of the toss. When your arms approach the top of the swing, they slow down like that coin. But they don't stop. On the way down, they gather momentum, just as the coin does, and reach maximum

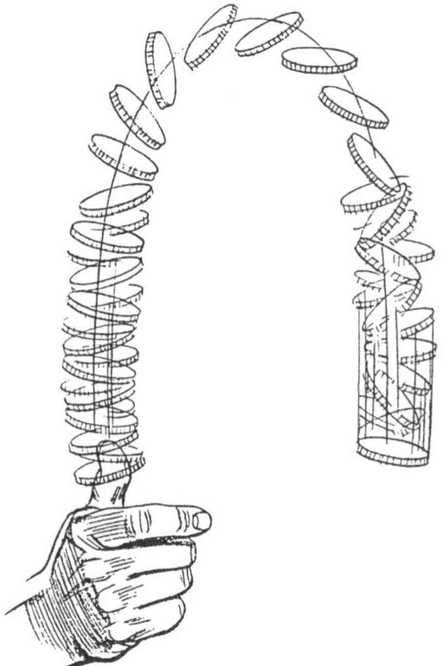

***Flip a coin***
*Your arms slow down as they approach and then descend from the top of your swing. Think of a coin slowly changing direction at the apex of its flip.*

speed just prior to impact. Slowing down at the top allows the different parts of your body to remain in sequence as they stop moving back and begin moving down. Stopping undermines the sequence by forcing all parts of the body to move down together. Your arms, legs and torso are all on slightly different schedules. It is futile to try to make them move as one.

## At the top

It is at the top of the backswing that the rhythm of your swing is most evident. Each swing is a kind of pulse. You should feel that same pulse from swing to swing. The pulse is the beat of the swing. It reveals itself most clearly at the end of the backswing and the beginning of the downswing. Watch the pros on the practice range. They each keep to their own individual beats, never hurrying, never varying.

An overly fast arm swing is like a drummer getting ahead of the band. It spoils the rhythm. Remember the drill we did earlier to find your optimum arm speed? Try it again now, swinging an iron club with your left arm only. Swing it back and forth, faster and faster, until it's going so fast the club and the hands pass the arm and the swing breaks down. Your optimum arm swing speed is the one just before the arm breaks down.

## Swinging down

The movement of the arms on the downswing will mirror their movement on the backswing. And just as the arms and hands reach the top slowly—like the coin—so they leave it slowly. Indeed, the slower your arms and hands begin the move down, the more time your feet and legs have to move into position to support them.

The shoulders are still merely followers of the arms, whose main job at this point is to protect and maintain the swinging motion of the clubhead. The rest of the body supports the arms. What the hands and arms do when they reach the top is to say, "Feet and legs, let's move again, we need your help. And we will go slowly to a point so that you will have time to get started."

You can see that the path of the arms on the downswing is slightly flatter than the path of the arms on the backswing. It is flatter because of the clearing of the lower body. If the arms and hands get too fast and the slower, heavier muscles of the lower body don't have time to begin their movement down and toward the target, they can't clear and

the arms are thrown outside their proper path. The club then comes "over the top," from outside the target line to inside it, creating a pull or a slice. If the arms stop at the top, and force the lower body to stop, too, the sequence is similarly ruined: All body parts start down together, and the faster arms and hands outrace the lower body and again come down "over the top," or from "outside to in."

The "inside path" teachers speak of is from inside the target line to along the target line to inside the target line again. It is the natural way to swing, because since you're standing on one side of the ball it's inefficient to deliver the club to the ball from the other side of the ball. It interferes with the centrifugal force the clubhead can generate.

**_Inside path_**
*Swinging from inside to along to inside the target line is the most natural and efficient way to swing.*

We'll talk more about path later. The important thing now is to create a free-swinging arm motion. It's easier if you think of yourself standing in the center of a giant arc, or semicircle, with the ball on the perimeter (see illustration). Your arms swing back and forth along that arc, and, as nearly as possible, you want to duplicate the backswing arc on the downswing. Ideally, you want the arc as wide as you can make it, because that makes it easier to repeat, swing to swing. (It also adds swing speed.) To maximize your arc, feel "wide" as you swing your arms back. Watch how your left arm extends naturally as you swing the club back.

## Impact

As you can see from the drawings, the position of your arms at impact nearly duplicates their position at address. The arms' job at address was to establish a position far enough from the body so that there is room now at impact for the lower body to turn out of the way, slide forward and straighten up. At the same time the arms must be relaxed enough to extend at impact. Davis says that when he has hit a really good shot he feels like his arms get six inches longer. Bob says he feels like his arms are chasing the ball. Whatever your sensation, remember that that extension is presaged at address. Unless your arms are hanging freely and devoid of tension, it can't happen.

Here is a simple exercise to give you the feel of the arms before and during impact. Pretend that there is a golf ball in front of you on the ground. Now throw an imaginary ball at that ball. You can try it with real balls outdoors. The exercise creates proper sequence of arm and body movement. Notice how the lower body naturally clears as the arm makes its throw? (Try another throw consciously trying to make the lower body clear, however, and it's disastrous.) Just absorb the feel of that throw. It will come back when you need it. If you find yourself out of sequence, go back and do this exercise.

## The flying elbow

Pay close attention to your elbows, especially if you feel you fight a "flying" right elbow. The fact is, proper arm motion on the backswing moves the elbow even farther away from the body than it was at address. And on the downswing the proper motion moves it back in toward the hip naturally. When you consciously try to keep your elbow pinned against your hip as a hedge against the flying elbow, you shrink the arc you created on the way to the top. The arm can't swing freely. If you let the right arm bend naturally, the right elbow will fold and set the club in the correct position, with the right thumb pointed at the right shoulder and directly under the shaft. Similarly, on the downswing, that natural movement of the elbow back toward the body cues the hands, wrists and forearms to start rotating to square the clubface at impact. Trying to hold the elbow in on either the backswing or the downswing undermines this natural motion.

## Following through

That folding of the arm on the backswing is repeated by the opposite arm on the follow-through. As your right arm folds swinging back, your left arm folds swinging through. One sure sign of a slice or pull swing is a rigid set of elbows.

Get the feel of proper arm motion now by swinging a club with one arm, while holding that forearm with your opposite hand so that your thumb rests on top of the forearm,

***Elbow fold***
*Your right elbow folds on the backswing. Your left folds on the follow-through. Get a feel for this motion by swinging an iron club in one arm while holding that forearm with your opposite hand. Switch arms. Later hit balls this way.*

your fingers on the underside of it (see illustration). Do it without a ball and then hitting a ball. Alternate arms.

Another way to check arm position is to monitor the position of the shaft, which should be either pointing at or lying parallel to the line of play at all times. After studying the positions, test this fact by creating a "line of play" or target line, using three or four clubs, a rope or even the edge of your carpet, and then slowly swinging a club through the positions in the drawings. When the swing begins, the clubhead end of the shaft points at the line of play. Halfway back the shaft is parallel to the line of play. As your arms approach the top of the swing the grip end of the shaft points at the line of play. At the top, the shaft again lies parallel to the line of play, etc.

This exercise points up the fact that the swing is both a swing and a lift. The arms swing the club back and then lift it over the shoulders. After impact, the feeling ought to be the same. As your hands release through the ball they rise, and the momentum of your hands rising lifts your arms. The hands and arms lead, the body follows.

Before you go on, test yourself again on the arm positions in the illustrations. Then begin swinging without a ball, with no other purpose but to feel that proper arm movement at each point in the swing. Finally, hit balls starting with hip-to-hip swings and progressing to full swings. Remember to make one practice swing for every ball you hit. And judge your swings not on ball flight at first but on your ability to create correct arm motion.

## Balance

Now that you've got the clubhead swinging, you're aware of another contributor to the ease and speed with which it swings: balance. Although your arms are not solely responsible for balance, they are a prime contributor because they set the pace and sequence of movement in your swing. A great way to test your balance during the swing is to swing with your eyes closed. Better yet, swing with a blindfold on, so you can't peek. If you're out of balance, you'll be off your feet. It's a fitting exercise with which to end this chapter. If, after studying the drawings and copying the positions, you are swinging with the kind of arm freedom Bob demonstrates in these drawings, try a dozen swings blindfolded. There is no better way to feel your new free-swinging arm motion.

## Your Game Plan

1. Gently swing a penknife from the end of a kerchief, creating an even motion so that the kerchief remains taut throughout the swing.

2. Holding the kerchief against the grip of an iron club, make left-arm swings while keeping the kerchief taut.

**3. The Swish Drill:** Swing a club back and forth, touching a spot on the floor or clipping a tee in the ground, striving for accuracy and freedom of arm movement.

### □□Creating Arm Motion

**1. Two-arm Swing:** Without a club, take your stance, align yourself to a target and swing your arms back and forth along the target line. Let them swing back farther and farther until your body gets into the act.

**2. Two-arm Swing with Clubs:** Holding an iron club in each hand, make two-arm swings at a target. Swing slowly, without letting the swing break down or the clubs cross one another.

**3. Arm Folding Exercise:** Swing a club with one arm at a time, holding the forearm of that arm with your opposite hand. (Place your "holding" thumb on top of the forearm, your fingers under it.) Notice the natural folding of the right arm on the backswing, the left on the follow-through.

**4. Left-arm-only Exercise:** Swing first an iron and then a wood with your left arm only, making slow swings at first and gradually increasing speed until the club passes your arm or the swing otherwise breaks down. The speed just before the breakdown is your optimum swing speed.

5. Learn the arm positions (pages 40-41) during the swing totally by feel and then hit balls while focusing on your arm movement, following steps A-E on page 11.

**6. Blindfold Exercise:** Swing a club, slowly at first, with your eyes closed or while wearing a blindfold. Let your arms swing freely and as fast as you can while maintaining your balance. Again, you will probably notice that your optimum swing speed is not as fast as you may have thought.

▽ ▽ ▽ ▽ ▽ ▽ ▽ ▽ ▽ ▽

# 5
# FEELING YOUR FEET

To get yourself in the mood for this chapter, stand up, pick out a line on your kitchen or living room floor, and pretend that you are a tightrope walker, suspended 50 feet above a circus ring, making your way across the hushed arena. Walk as slowly and as carefully as you need to keep one foot after another on the "rope." Really do it. "Feel" the rope under your feet, between your toes, which are gripping it, reacting to the subtle shift of your weight from one side to another. Notice how your feet work together with your outstretched hands to find and maintain your balance.

Now change the scene. You're not a tightrope walker any longer; you're Fred Astaire. You're wearing a top hat and tails, dancing across a glistening white marble floor. The big band is playing "Puttin' on the Ritz" and you are moving, as if on weightless rollers, from one end of the room to the other. With your hands and arms outstretched you are lighter than sound, lighter than air. Your feet absorb the beat, they use it to create rhythm, to keep you in balance.

If the keynote of the Arms Chapter was "freedom," the bywords of this one are rhythm and balance: The grounded balance of the tightrope walker. The weightless rhythm of the dancer. Your feet are your source of rhythm and balance. When they don't work correctly, your golf swing is no swing at all. You are Fred Astaire in combat boots.

We said earlier that if you read and worked on no other

chapter but the one on Hands, your swing would improve immeasurably. This chapter ranks a close second. If you did the tightrope exercise above you noticed how closely the hands, arms and feet work together. That's true of almost any athletic endeavor. Take a baseball pitcher. He delivers the pitch with his hand, but pushes off the rubber with his foot. Without the coordination of the two, no amount of body motion would propel the pitch fast enough. The shot putter, the tennis player, the pole vaulter, the sprinter all combine hand-arm motion with feet movement to generate speed and power—and to maintain balance as they do. In golf, your hands—and arms—create the swinging motion. Your feet control the rhythm of the swing and keep you in balance. The great Bobby Jones knew that. He practiced hit-

***Bobby's drill***
*The great Bobby Jones improved his footwork and balance by hitting shots with his feet together. Try it yourself, beginning with hip-to-hip swings with a short iron.*

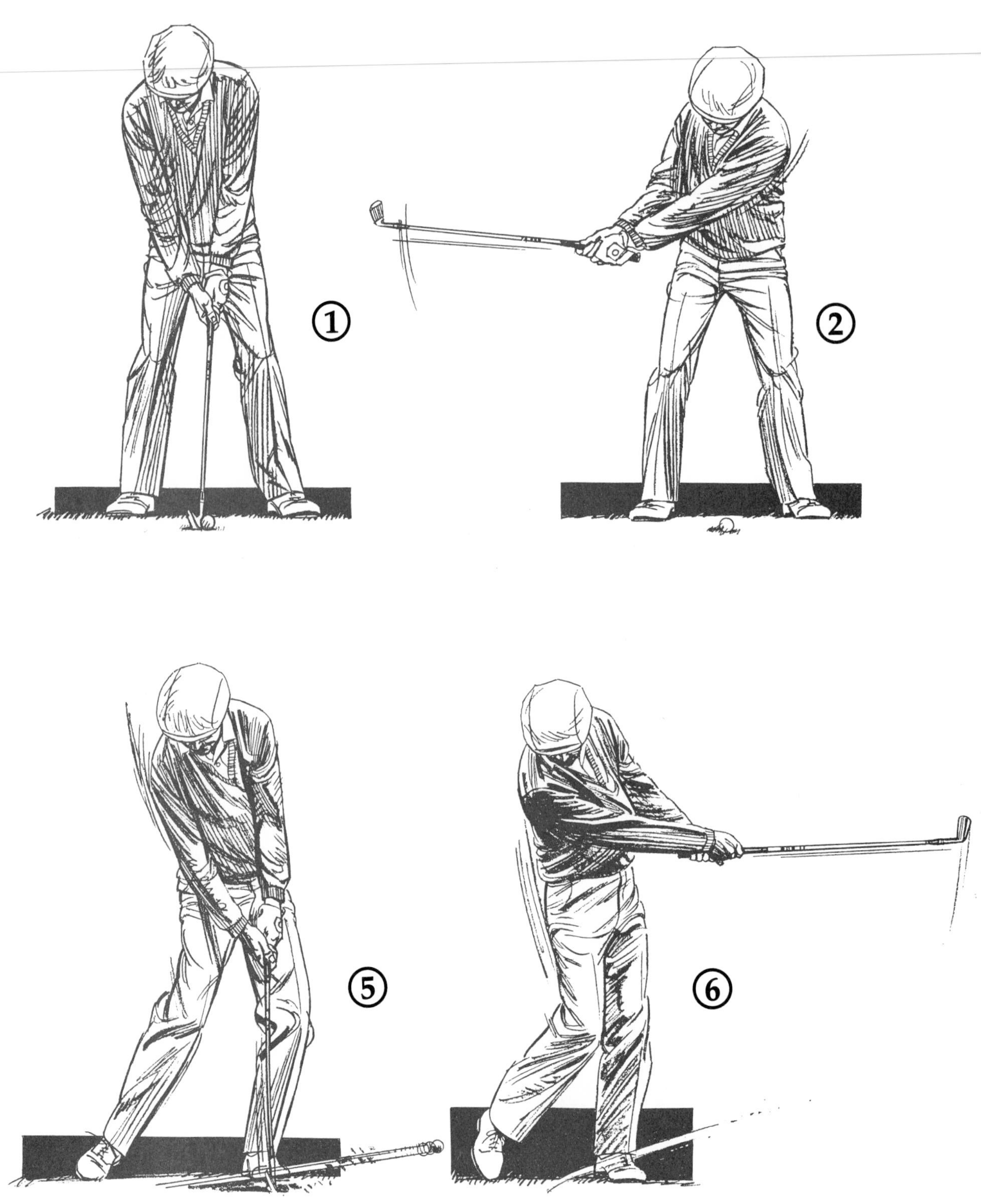
①
②
⑤
⑥

## Your Feet

The masters of rhythm and balance, your feet rank second only to your hands in their influence on your swing.

ting shots with his feet together to perfect his rhythm and balance.

When, after studying the drawings, you begin to swing the club, let your feet naturally support the movement of your hands and arms. There is less to DO in this chapter than previous ones because much of what you do with your feet is instinctive. The exercises in this chapter will help you isolate and feel those instinctive movements so that you will more easily repeat them.

## Address

At address Bob's feet are positioned slightly outside his knees. We'd recommend that you experiment a bit with the width of your stance, as well as with the angle your feet approach the line of play. Bob's stance is a little bit wider than normal, which is appropriate for him because he has unusually quick legs and feet. In general, a narrower stance encourages more turn and footwork. If you get your feet too wide at address, you will find it hard to activate your feet. The amateur players we've worked with tend to widen their stances too much on the longer clubs in an effort to get leverage for that longer swing. The problem is, they frequently take their feet and legs out of the swing by getting their stances too wide.

***Walk in***
*At address, set your feet at the angles they fall when you walk. From there, experiment.*

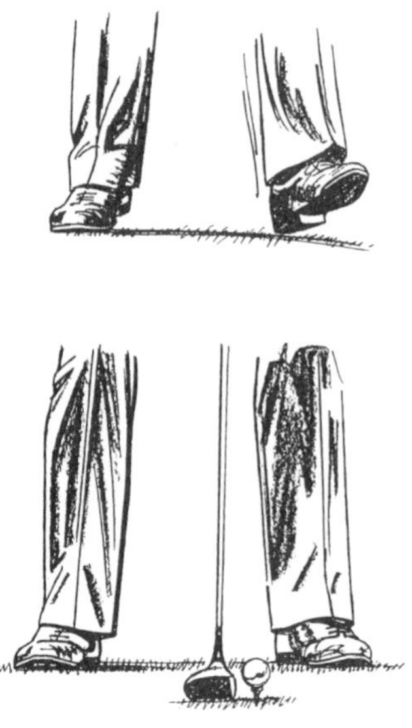

We suggest you start with your ankles directly underneath your hips. That should allow you to swing freely and in balance. If you have a difficult time maintaining your balance, try a slightly wider stance. But the general rule is keep your feet as close together as possible while still maintaining your balance during a full swing. When you lose balance, or feel that your legs can't participate in the swing, experiment with a wider or narrower stance.

Notice that Bob's right foot is "square" to the target line; that is, it is perpendicular to that line. Again, this is fine for the supple player, but we'd recommend the less agile player start with the right foot angled to the right slightly. (Never angle either foot in toward the ball; that's death.) The left foot is also angled out. Bob's position is fine for most players. Some of you will want that angle even wider. A good starting point is to set your feet at the angles they're at when you walk. From there, experiment.

There was a time when teachers recommended that you start with your weight back on your heels. It was not great advice then and it still isn't today. For years Bob and Davis have taught students to start with the weight on the balls of their feet. Bob's weight, distributed equally on each foot, rests mostly on the balls of his feet, with some going toward his toes. He's in what we call an "athletic ready" position. It's the position of a tennis player awaiting his opponent's serve or a linebacker waiting for the snap of the ball. If your weight is on your heels you are not ready to move. You'll be unable to make a full turn because you'll lose your balance.

## Heel check

A good way to check that you have your weight distributed properly is to alternate lifting your heels slightly, feeling the weight on the inside of the opposite foot from the one that is lifted. If your weight is too far toward your heels, you won't be able to lift them. Instead you'll automatically lift your toes. We see a lot of players with too much weight on their heels. Watch good golfers just before they swing. They're finding the beat of their swings by lifting those heels just a little bit.

Your weight should lie slightly toward the insides of your feet for ease of weight shift while maintaining balance. If your weight rests on the outside of your left foot, for example, you will first have to shift the weight to the inside of that foot before you can shift it to the right.

Foot position is critical because it frees your feet, legs and lower body to support the movement of the hands and arms. If your feet can't respond, ultimately your body can't respond. Your body will fight the natural motion of your swing. As Bob says, "You need traction to control action."

## Swinging back

As his hands and arms move the club away from the ball, Bob's weight is shifting ever so slightly from the inside of his left foot to the inside of his right foot. The first evidence of this is the rolling—not lifting—of his left foot away from the target, pushing his ankle inward and his left knee toward his right knee. As long as the club is moving rearward, the left foot rolls but the heel does not lift. The heel doesn't come up until the arms have quit swinging to the right and started to swing around and up. The heel is pulled off the ground, never lifted. It responds to the left ankle, which bends in as the arms are going sideways, and as the arms go up, lifts and pulls the heel with it. If your feet are picking up the rhythm of your arms going back, you will feel that left heel being tugged up.

## At the top

As the club moves upward to the top of the swing the weight moves from the front of the right foot to the heel of the right foot.

Then the process reverses itself. The weight moves from the heel to the toes and from the middle to the inside. (The knees, which we will talk more about later, help move the weight to the inside of the right foot so that it can push off as the club enters the hitting area.)

**_Heel check_**
*Your left foot should return on the downswing to the spot it vacated on the backswing. Slightly closer to the target is fine; farther away is not.*

The left heel, which has been lifted, ideally returns to its original spot. If the left heel returns to a spot slightly targetward, that's fine. If it slides away from the target, however, it will encourage both a loss of balance and an outside-to-inside downswing (see illustration).

The inside of the left foot touches the ground first, a reverse of how it was pulled off the ground.

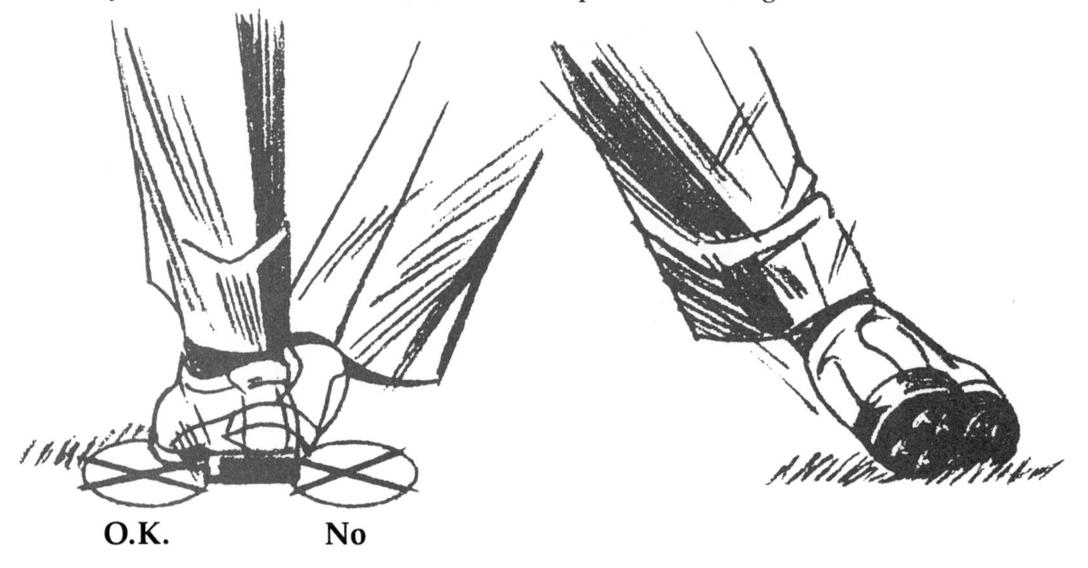


## Impact

As the club approaches impact, Bob's weight, predominantly on his right foot, moves left until it rests equally on both feet. The weight on his right foot has moved from the heel toward the toes. At impact, the weight is equally distributed between the two feet, but well on the toes of both. The right leg is flexed and the right knee now is pointed toward the target, evidence that Bob has pushed off his right foot.

The weight of his left foot, on his toes at impact, will move quickly toward the heel of that foot. At the same time, the weight is shifting from inside the left foot to outside it.

That allows the left knee to move toward the target, sliding the foundation of the swing forward. (More later, in the Legs Chapter.)

## Finding your feet

That's the ideal. How do you get your feet and ankles to respond with the same kind of quickness and strength? How do you keep them from lagging behind or getting ahead of your hands and arms? There aren't a lot of exercises for the feet. Teachers have long believed that good footwork is instinctive and found it hard to teach. The best exercises for footwork are not golf exercises at all but activities such as dancing and aerobics, activities that combine flexibility with rhythmic movement. The first thing you can do to improve your footwork, therefore, aside from studying the accompanying drawings, is to ask your physician for a program to improve your flexibility and balance. Dancing is excellent because it combines footwork with lateral and rotary movements not unlike those in the swing.

Beyond that, one of the best exercises ever created to foster foot (and leg) movement is one created by Wild Bill Mehlhorn, one of the premier ball-strikers of the 1930s and 1940s. Mehlhorn took a club, laid it across his thighs as he stood, and held it there with his arms at full length while he began to "swing" (see illustration). Try it, moving your legs

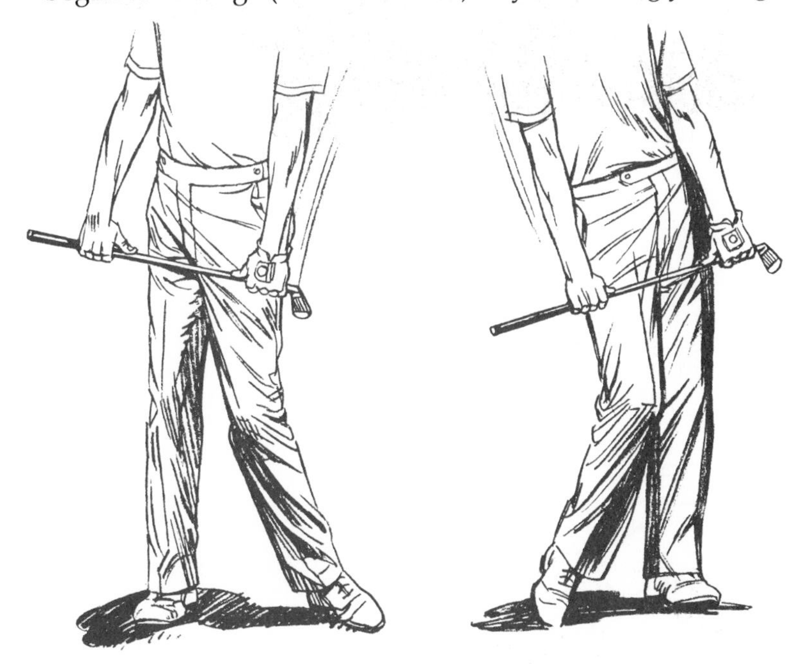

***Mehlhorn Drill***
*Lay a club across your thighs and make swinging motions, keeping the club against your body. Feel your feet controlling your leg movement and weight shift.*

### Ball under shaft

*Holding a club vertical with your left hand, throw a ball between your body and the shaft. Feel how your feet work as you "wind up," push off and throw. The throwing motion mirrors that of the swing.*

as if you were swinging, but keeping the shaft pressed against your thighs. Not as easy as it looks, is it? As you get better and better at it, you'll begin to feel the proper weight shift within and between your feet.

Notice how easy it is, however, to get out of sync, usually when you're trying to move too quickly. As long as you don't allow your legs to get ahead of your feet, you will have no trouble keeping that shaft against your thighs. Once legs or hips take over, you lose "traction" and then balance. It's very much like the arms-shoulders relationship. Let the shoulders rule and you'll rue it.

Another excellent footwork exercise is throwing a ball under a shaft (see illustration). Stand a club up and hold it in place with your left hand. Now throw a ball in the space between your body and the shaft. As you throw, feel your weight moving toward the throwing arm, and then moving back in the direction of and in support of the throw. Notice how natural pushing off the insteps of your feet is when you're throwing; it should be the same when you're swinging.

Swinging a club while standing on one leg is another good drill. For some of you this will be a challenge. The trick is to make very easy mini-swings, feeling your weight move from one side of your foot to the other. Try it first on your left leg and then on your right. Make a full swing, come back to address, make another, etc. See if you can make 20 swings this way. Then switch legs.

When you have no trouble keeping your balance while swinging on one leg, start a swing on your right leg and step left as you swing. Set up as you would to hit a shot, on both legs. Then lift the left leg, take the club back standing only on your right foot and on the downswing step into the left-foot position you vacated. Make 20 or 30 swings like this.

When you can do this drill consistently without losing your balance, hit balls this way—off a tee. It's a good idea, when you do the Step-in Drill, to mark the position of your left foot with chalk or paint before you start so that you step back into exactly the same foot position you left. Remember to alternate between hitting balls off one leg and making normal swings, five or 10 balls of each.

By the time you've done a few repetitions of this drill, you'll begin feeling your ankles—and they'll feel sore. It's often weak ankles that lead to balance problems. The best

***Step-in drill***
*Set up as you would to hit an iron shot. As you start to take the club back, lift your left foot. On the downswing step back into the spot you vacated and hit the shot. It's a good idea to mark your left foot position to be sure you return to it.*

exercise we know for strengthening ankles is the one skating coaches gave us as kids: Walk on the insides of your feet, so that the outsides of your shoes are off the ground. It may be tough on your shoes, but do it enough and you'll notice that the footwork we recommend comes a lot easier.

## Your Game Plan

**1. The Mehlhorn Drill.** With your arms fully extended, place a club across your thighs and move your feet and legs as you would during a swing. Remember to keep the club against your legs.

2. Throw a ball between your body and a shaft held vertical by your left hand. Notice how the left foot and then the right pushes off.

**3. The Step-in Drill.** Set up as you would to hit an iron shot. On the backswing lift your left foot. As you do, take the club back standing only on your right foot. On the downswing step back into the spot you vacated and hit the shot.

4. Get to know the feel of your legs during the swing by studying the sequential drawings on pages 58-59 and following steps A-E on page 11.

# 6
# FEELING YOUR LEGS

When a boxer drives home an uppercut, he pushes forward off his back leg and slides a flexed front leg in front of him to support the punch. A baseball pitcher, firing a fastball, kicks off his back leg and stretches his front one far forward to balance himself and support the throw. A basketball player cushions every dribble with flexed knees and supple legs.

But the legs are forgotten. The boxer has "a great right." The pitcher, "a live arm." The basketball player, "quick hands." And so it is in golf. Golfers are said to have fast hands or quick hands, quick wrists, powerful forearms, a great shoulder turn, sometimes even good footwork. But seldom are they praised for knee action or leg drive. And yet, next to hands, feet and possibly arms, the legs are the most influential contributors to the swing.

Leg action is little talked about partly because many players—and teachers—don't understand it. Even very good players have a hard time describing what they do with their legs. Some don't think about them, having learned leg and footwork instinctively. Others don't because they concentrate on arm swing, and find it impossible to monitor leg movement, too.

In this chapter we'll describe leg action in more detail, we suspect, than you've heard or read before. But we caution you not to confuse, as Seymour Dunn put it, "something that happens with something you have to do." We'll give you drills to allow you to feel proper leg action without having to think about it as you swing. Before that, we'll describe what the legs do during the swing so that you don't develop habits that interfere with their proper movement.

The legs have three functions. Their first function is to support. (Think of the tubular frame holding the girl on the swing.) Their second function is to balance. (As with the baseball pitcher.) And their third function is to add speed to the centrifugal force created by the hands and arms. (Much like the boxer, multiplying the power of his punch with good leg drive.) Again, support, balance and speed.

Without your legs' support, your upper body gets out of sync; you lose balance, you are not grounded, have no pillar to push off and, therefore, no power. Repeat the drill we introduced in the Feet Chapter, but now feel the movement of your legs. Holding a club vertical with your left hand,

***Good legs***
*Strong leg drive is as essential to a golfer as it is to a baseball pitcher.*

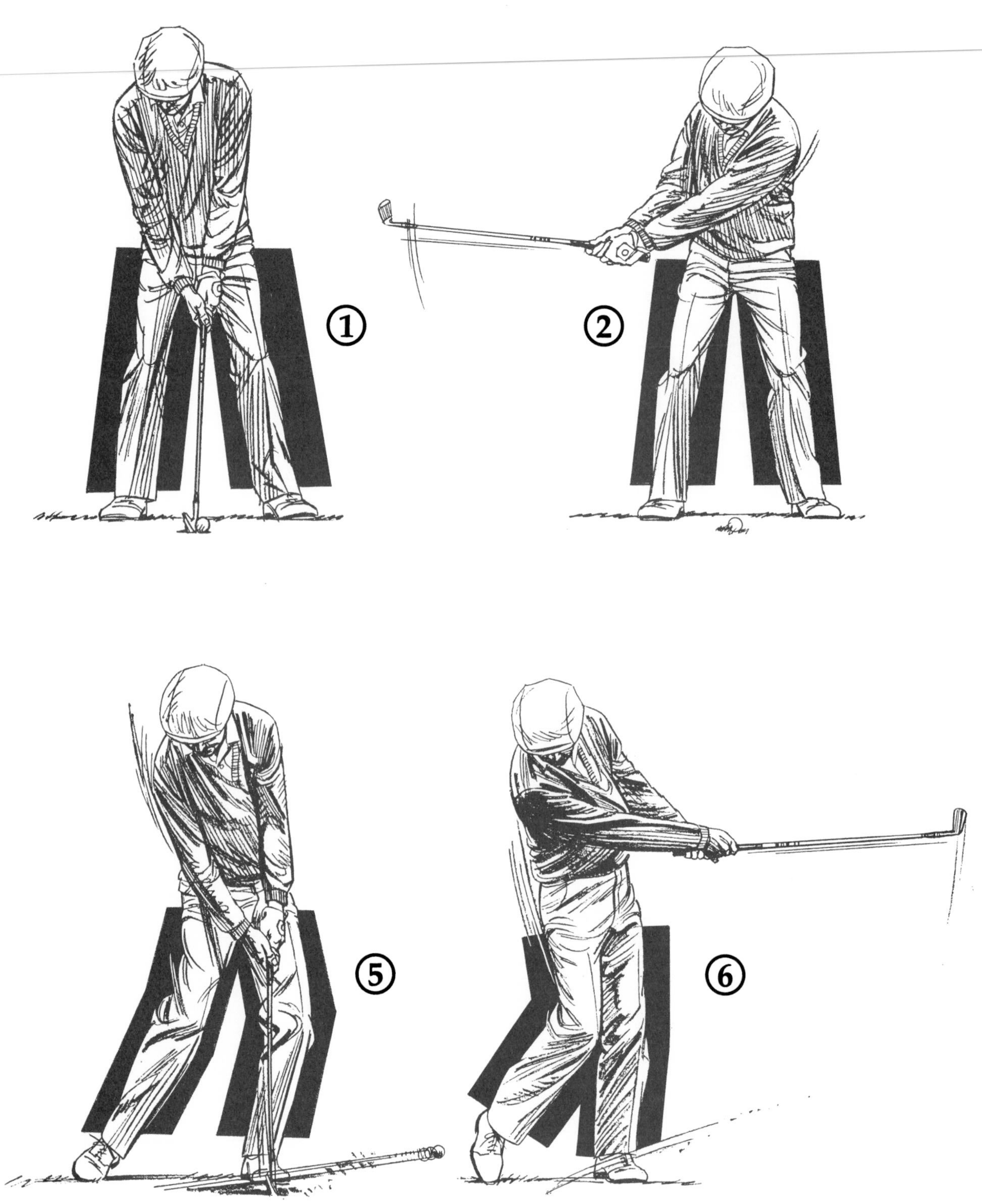
①
②
⑤
⑥

# Your Legs

Often overlooked, your legs support, balance and add speed to your golf swing.

throw a ball under it with your right. When you do this drill you are forced to use your legs to support the motion of your arm. If you make hard throws, increase the speed of your delivery and don't move your legs to support the throw, you'll also learn something about balance. You'll lose it. Or take a tennis ball and throw it sidearm at a spot on a wall or at another ball lying on the ground. Notice how you naturally stride forward to balance yourself and support the throw. Try it a few more times, adding zip as you go. Can you feel how your legs contribute to the additional speed?

These three functions—support, balance and speed—are incorporated in two different kinds of leg action: rotary and lateral. Put another way, the legs both turn and slide. Confusion about the relative importance of these two actions, we think, has led to misteaching about the correct use of the legs. You've probably been encouraged to use your legs and

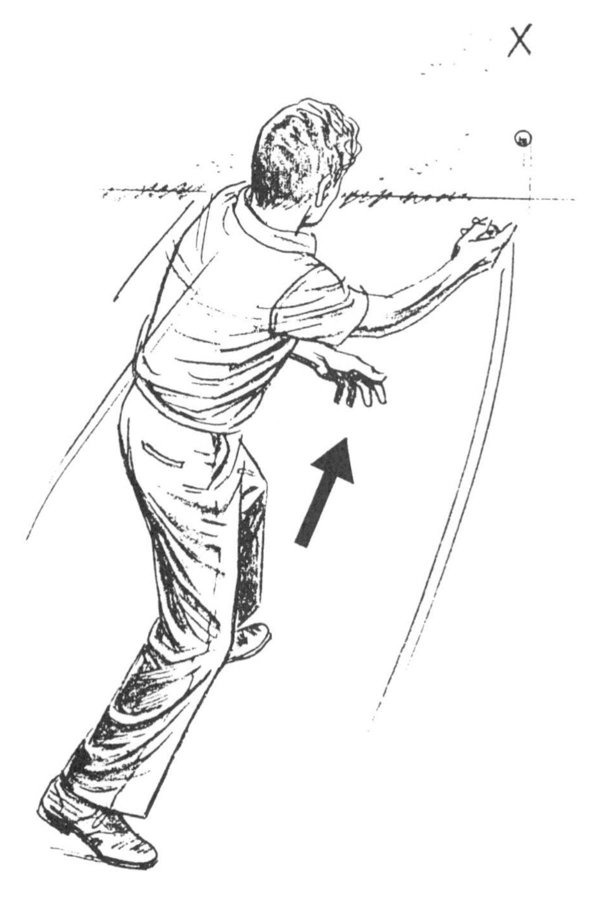


***Wall toss***
*Toss a ball at a wall, varying the distance and speed of your throws. Notice how your legs instinctively adjust to the different throws, adding speed and support, just as they do with your golf shots.*

hips to turn, to create rotary movement. But you've probably been discouraged from using them to slide, to create lateral movement. That's swaying, you've been told, the opposite of a good hip turn. It's our contention that of the two kinds of leg movement, lateral is the most important, and that the lack of punch in many amateur swings results from too much emphasis on rotary movement. In their concentration on the rotary action players fail to acknowledge the need for lateral movement.

Obviously we believe in a good turn, and we will teach you leg exercises to improve your turn. But we also believe that you can overdo it. Remember the old tip, "Swing in a barrel"? Look at the drawings of Bob's swing and consider what would happen to a barrel if it were fitted around him before he took the club back. As a boy, Bob tried that tip with a real barrel, his family's, emptied of apples. When he finished swinging there was no barrel to put the apples back into. It was shattered when Bob knocked it over, with him inside, at the finish of his swing. The barrel kept him

***Bob's barrel***
*Bob's leg-drive shatters the myth of "swinging in a barrel." The swing is more than just a turn; it's a slide and a twist, too.*

from moving his legs laterally to support his arms and hands, to balance himself.

The two kinds of movement, lateral and rotary, complement one another. Too often, the rotary is made to dominate. One of the reasons that it comes to dominate is that golfers are taught to control the lower-body movement with their hips, when actually it is the legs that control. The hips take their lead from the legs, not the other way around. It's very much like the relationship of the shoulders to the arms. Just as the arms created the shoulder turn, so the legs create the hip turn. Hip movement (and your leg movement as a whole) is predominantly rotary on the backswing, but mainly lateral, side to side, on the downswing.

Take a moment and do these two exercises: First, stand without a club in your address position. Now turn your hips as far as you can, around and back again. Second, take the same stance, but instead of turning, swing your left leg back past your right and then step forward with your left foot into the spot it vacated (see illustration). During which exercise did you feel more in balance, more secure on your feet? We guess the second. Because in the second exercise the motion was a combination of lateral and rotary. It's that feeling we want you to cultivate. The first exercise, on the other hand, emphasized turn over slide, robbing you of balance. Do the second drill, which we call the Motion Exercise, again and again. When you can do it without losing balance, switch legs. The exercise not only fosters better balance, but demonstrates how much of a lateral movement you can tolerate without losing balance.

Overemphasis on turn and on generating that turn from the hips, hurts in another way: It takes your knees out of the swing. As you can see in the drawings of Bob on pages 70-71, his knees lead. He said once that the only thing he feels during his swing are his arms and his knees. Obviously his arms and hands are the leaders of swing, but he uses his knees to get his lower body to follow their lead. Look at the left knee as he begins to take the club back. It points back, away from the target, in the direction the hands and arms are taking the club. It follows their lead to the point of passing the ball on the backswing. Now look at the knees at the point of impact. With the knees flexed, the left knee is farther forward than any part of Bob's body, pointing toward the target, helping to support and cushion the shot,

***Motion exercise***
*Without a club, take your stance and swing your left foot past your right (not just to it, as you did in the Step-in Drill), replanting it on your downswing. Do it until it's easy to maintain your balance. Switch legs.*

just as the boxer supports his blow with his flexed lead knee. If you move your hands and arms forward to swing the club forward, there has to be something below them to support that movement. If the lower-body movement at impact is *around* (a turn, led by the left hip) instead of *forward* (a slide, led by the left knee and leg), you've removed your support system. It has left the target line, where it's needed, while your hands and arms deliver the club to the ball with no support. You're spinning out or bailing out, the bane of many a weekend slicer. Yes, your hips will eventually turn to the left, just as they turned to the right. But that turn will occur later—naturally.

"But wait a minute," some of you may be saying. "Without that hip turn at impact, how will the arms catch up with the lower body? How will the hands be able to square the clubface?" The answer is that your hands are capable of moving and turning so fast that there is no danger they won't catch up. What's more, the longer you delay the rotary action, the greater the force of your swing at impact. The arms will catch up and the hands will square up the clubface provided the lower body moves to support them. If the lower body moves off the line; that is, if it turns too early, you'll pull the rug out from under your arms and

***Pulling the rug***
*A premature hip turn away from the ball at impact removes your support system, in effect pulling the rug out from under you. The longer you delay that rotary action, the greater the force of your swing.*

hands. Overdoing the turn will cause you to come into the ball from outside the target line and either pull it or pull-slice it. You can overdo the lateral movement, too, and that will send the ball straight right. But we suspect that the former fault is the more common one.

As you study the leg positions in the drawing, note when the leg movement has been lateral and when it's been rotary. Notice the sequence of movement. Simplified, it's a turn, a slide and then a little turn, almost a twist. The better you know the movements, the less apt you will be to undermine them by overemphasizing one kind of leg action over another.

# Leg positions during the swing

## Address

Both turn and slide are presaged—or prevented—at address, and both depend on leg "mobility," the readiness to move when the hands and arms say, "Let's go!"

Proper stance and leg posture create mobility. The enemy of mobility, just as with the arm swing, is tension; it "freezes" your legs. If your legs are tense, they won't move when your arms move on the backswing. They will tend to slide too much going back and turn too much coming through. They will be unable to create the supportive "undercarriage" at impact that the arms and hands require. So the first rule of good legwork is stay relaxed at address.

Balance reduces tension. Dividing your weight equally between your legs at address, as Bob has, and flexing your knees slightly, keep your legs in an "athletic ready" posture. If you place your weight predominantly on one leg or the other, that leg becomes tense because it must hold a body that is essentially out of balance. If you do not flex your knees, they also become tense because it's harder for them to stay in balance. Either way, your legs can't "go" when your arms say "go" at the start of the backswing. They're too worried about keeping you from falling over. On the other hand, if you flex your knees too much at address, you also create tension in your thighs. A good rule of thumb is, position your kneecaps directly over the balls of your feet at address.

Notice that Bob's legs are not pinched in at address, another habit that creates tension. Not too long ago an LPGA pro called Davis and said, "My right elbow is out of position and I am moving off the ball." Davis couldn't understand how it was happening and so he invited the pro

***Knee position***
*Flex your legs so that your kneecaps are directly over the balls of your feet.*

**No pinching**
*Pinching your legs in at address produces tension in your legs, preventing natural leg movement on the backswing. Position your legs about shoulder width at address, with the weight evenly distributed between the two.*

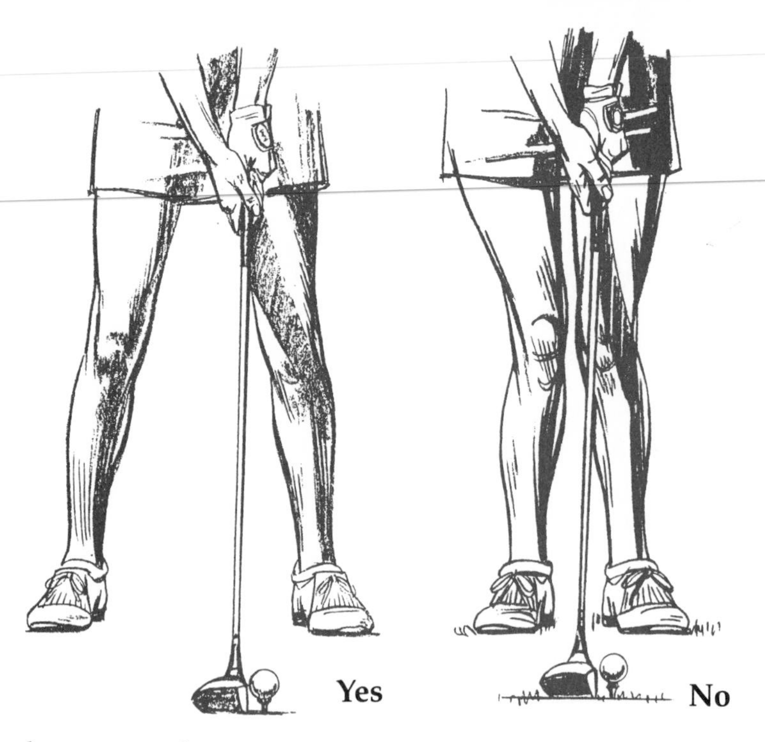


down to see him at Sea Island, Ga., where he teaches. As soon as he saw her setup, he diagnosed the problem. By pinching her knees in at address, she had loaded her legs with tension and made it impossible for them to turn on the backswing. That threw everything else out of whack.

Bob sets his legs very wide apart at address, because he has unusually quick legs and feet. You can probably set up with your legs a bit closer together than his, with your feet about as wide apart as your shoulders. That will make it easier for your legs to keep up with your hands and arms.

You can test your balance at address by having a friend give you a gentle push after you take your address position. Give him permission to do it when you're not expecting it, from any direction he chooses. If you're in an "athletic ready" position, you should recover immediately. If not, you may be on your backside.

## Swinging back

In the first quarter of the swing, from address to the point when the club is parallel to the ground on the backswing, leg movement is not dramatic. The left knee moves away from the target a few inches, to a point opposite the ball. As weight shifts to the right side, the right knee loses some, but not all, of its flex and supports the additional weight. So far, hip turn has not been great. But it has been enough to allow the hands and arms to swing the club back while the body stays in balance.

From halfway through the backswing to the top of the swing, leg movement is much more marked and it is mostly a turn. At the top, Bob's left knee is several inches behind the ball. His right knee, still not straight—it never will lose its flex entirely—has turned off the target line. Because the right leg was flexed and "ready" at address, it easily accepts the additional weight while still being able to lead the right hip around. Notice, though, how the right leg braces directly under the upper body. The weight is never allowed to shift outside the leg, even though as much as 90 percent of the body's weight is now resting on the right side.

## Swinging down

On the downswing, as it did on the backswing, the left knee leads in creating lower-body support for the onrushing arms and hands. The knees widen as the left knee slides toward the target and the right knee moves back toward the line of play. At the point where the hands are hip high and ready to begin to deliver the clubhead to the ball, the left knee is back where it was at address, several inches targetward of the ball. Together, the knees have widened and moved forward the "platform" on which the rest of the body rests. Since the arms will be delivering the club not just to but well past the ball, the legs must also slide beyond the ball to support that action. By the time the hands descend to a hip-high position, the right knee has finished its movement back to the line and is beginning to follow the left knee along the line to the target. As the gap between them widens, the right leg pushes off the right foot and thrusts the right knee forward so that by impact, it has returned to within a few inches of the ball. The player feels his feet and legs pressing downward and forward.

These drawings are based on a 5-iron swing. Because an iron club is descending as it strikes the ball—as opposed to a wood club, which is level or ascending—the movement of the knees is also slightly downward. With a driver, knee movement would be less downward and more lateral.

Pay particular attention to the movement of Bob's hips during this phase of the swing. From a "coiled" position at the top, they are turned by the legs to a square position by the time the hands reach hip level, and the right knee has made its way back to the line of play. From that point until impact, the hip movement is more slide than turn, following the lead of the sliding legs.

## Impact

At impact, the left knee has traveled six to eight inches past the ball—as far as it can go—and the right knee has reached a point a few inches behind the ball. Both point toward the target. Now, with the club delivered square to the ball, the weight rests entirely on the left leg, which, to allow the club to travel along the target line as it strikes through the ball, must clear out of the way. To accomplish that clearing, the left leg moves off the target line, taking the left hip with it, in a shortened turn, or twist. By the time the hands reach a point hip high, the left leg is nearly straight, and the right leg "chases" the club down the target line. Notice, though, that the straightening of the left leg does not occur until well after impact and after the hands and clubhead have passed the body. Straightening the leg too quickly causes the hip to pull away from the target line prematurely, inducing a "spinout" or "bailout" and a nasty slice.

One teacher said that good players play well "beneath themselves," and these drawings depict what he had in mind. The legs, supporting the hands and arms and led by the knees, have turned back and then shifted forward, well beyond Bob's swing center. What's important, however, is that the swing center—the base of Bob's neck—has not moved. As the legs slide, they add velocity to the downswing. The swing center remains in place. The knees are flexed, like two arrows pointing to the target, at impact. Many golfers don't accomplish this because they're afraid to slide sideways. Challenge yourself to feel that slide. If your swing center stays in place, you can slide your legs and lower body toward the target almost as much as you want. That's swinging and moving well "beneath yourself," i.e., below your waist.

## Following through

The release of the club, and the velocity with which it comes through the ball, will tell you when it's time to end the slide and start to turn. Actually, you won't have any choice. It will happen automatically. But if you are going to complement the speed of your arms, wrists and hands as they bring the club down and forward, you must keep the rest of your anatomy moving forward. Don't worry about how much you turn at this point.

We mentioned earlier the fear of some students that this slide will not allow the hands to catch up to the lower body and thus leave the clubface open at impact. Study the drawings and you can see that it's really not a problem. Even Bob's unusually quick lower body can't outrace his hands and arms. They will not be able to catch up, however, if the left hip and the left shoulder are doing nothing but rotating. If they are rotating as fast as they are capable, the hands never catch up, because that rotation causes you to pull on the handle and leave the clubhead behind. If you are moving sideways—and not around—at impact, however, you have all the flexibility and speed in your hands to

***Timing frame***
*Are your arms and legs in sync? Test them by "walking" slowly through your swing motion while facing a door frame. Ideally, the shaft will enter the hitting area flush against the wall. If the grip end leads and the shaft hits the edge of the wall, you may be "spinning out," turning your hips away from the ball too soon.*

square the clubface when the time comes. Here's a way to check it. Stand at address in a doorway with your clubshaft flat against the wall in front of you. Make a slow-motion swing back and down, returning the club to its position against the wall. (See previous illustration.) If your hands or the shaft hit the door frame before the club returns to square you have probably turned your left hip to the left too soon.

## Making it natural

As we said earlier, the fact that something happens, in this case with the legs, doesn't necessarily mean you have to do something to make it happen. Let's go back to the Motion Exercise we did earlier. It will teach you most of the movement in the drawings. It's especially useful for those of you who've been hanging back on your left sides because you are afraid of "swaying" or have just never really felt your legs move during a swing.

Take your address position without a club. Swing your left foot over your right and then back into its original position. After you've done the Motion Exercise for a while without a club, swing an iron club. You'll see that your left leg naturally picks up the rhythm of the hands and arms on the backswing, and the hands and arms naturally pick up the rhythm of the left leg on the downswing. After a while, hit balls while doing it. If you're like the students we've seen over the years, you'll be grinning about how well you can hit a ball this way.

***More motion***
*Return to the motion exercise, this time swinging an iron club and hitting shots.*

Another leg drill: To experience the tremendous support your legs provide your arm swing, play 10- to 20-yard 7-iron shots from a tee, generating most of your motion with your legs. Have the feeling that you're hitting the shots entirely with your legs. Make sure your arms, hands and wrists are all reacting to your feet and legs, the opposite of what usually occurs. (If you've become too wristy with your chipping and have "chili-dipped" a few lately, this exercise will cure you. It's not a bad way to chip.)

Exercises like these also help you to find a swing pace that will allow hands-arms and legs-feet to work harmoniously. The sequence of movements that may seem complicated when we describe them begins to occur naturally, and the overemphasis on one particular movement—such as the hip turn—will no longer undermine and destroy that sequence.

## Your Game Plan

**1. The Address Push.** Take your address position and ask a friend to push you from one direction or another. You want to be so balanced that a gentle push doesn't throw you off.

**2. Study Leg Positions.** Holding an iron club, put yourself through the swing positions on pages 70-71 with special attention to your legs. Check your legwork in a mirror, following steps A-E on page 11.

**3. Turn Versus Slide Test.** Taking an address position without a club, make as big a turn as you can. Next, from the same stance, lift your left leg off the ground and swing it past your right leg. Then swing it back, feeling your body slide left as the leg returns to its original spot. Which offers more balance, creates more turn? We bet the second exercise.

**4. Motion Exercise.** Lift your left foot and swing it past your right, replanting it in its original position on the downswing. Do it first without a club and ball, then with. When you go to the range, hit balls doing the Motion Exercise after marking your left foot position with chalk or paint.

**5. Leg Shots.** Hit 10- to 20-yard 7-iron shots, using almost no arm or hand motion. Feel as though you're propelling the ball entirely with your legs. Start with the ball teed, then hit some balls from the turf.

**6. Return-to-square Drill.** Stand at address in a doorway with your club flat against the wall in front of you. Make a slow-motion swing back and down, returning the club to its position against the wall. If your hands or the shaft hit the door frame before the club returns to square, you have probably turned your left hip to the left too soon.

# 7

# FEELING YOUR TRUNK

We might dedicate this chapter to football's middle linebacker. Consider the linebacker's stance: Spine tilted slightly forward so that his weight is distributed equally on the balls of his feet; legs, arms, torso ready but relaxed, capable of moving forward, backward, left or right when the ball is snapped. Consider, also, his function: response. He does not call the play, as a quarterback would, or lead the play like a blocking guard or tackle. He does not carry the ball or take a fake handoff to provide a "decoy." He responds solely to the movement of the football, whether run or pass, left or right, deep or short. Overactive linebackers, linebackers who guess pass too often or lean left one too many times, get burned. They're caught off balance, left in the lurch, or led into a trap.

So it is with your trunk, or torso—that portion of your anatomy from the hip joints to the shoulder joints. It's job is only to respond to the movement of your hands and arms on the one hand and your legs on the other. Although it will come as a surprise to those of you who have worked long and hard on your "pivot," your trunk is no more a leader in the swing than your shoulders or hips are. The trunk follows. The trunk responds. The trunk reacts. It initiates nothing, either on the backswing or the downswing. If you remember nothing else in this chapter, remember that and you've remembered a lot.

The linebacker image is apt here for another reason. The

linebacker's stance is an "athletic ready" stance, and the spine angle of that stance is a model for trunk posture at address. Spine angle is a forgotten fundamental of golf, and yet spinal posture sets the stage for the swing. It either allows or prevents a proper turn and a proper sequence of hand, arm, leg and foot motion. These are the elements necessary for proper posture: The spine must be straight, not hunched over. It must be at a right angle to the target line, and it must lean toward the line at an angle that's appropriate for the player's body type and club being hit. Paul Runyan uses a piece of wire to demonstrate the importance of the first element to his students. First he takes the wire, absolutely straight, sticks it into the ground and turns it with his fingers. The wire turns, but stays in the same space. Then he bends the wire, sticks it into the ground and turns it. This time the top of the wire moves to one side and the other as it is being turned. It's a simple but vivid illustration of what happens to a golfer's head—and swing center—as a result of poor posture. If your spine is straight, however, it is easy to swing around a stable center.

Besides being straight, the spine must also be perpendicular to the line of play; that is, it should not tilt to one side or the other.

***Like a linebacker***
*Emulate the linebacker's athletic posture: His spine is straight, not hunched or curled. His weight is on the balls of his feet. His head is up. He's ready.*

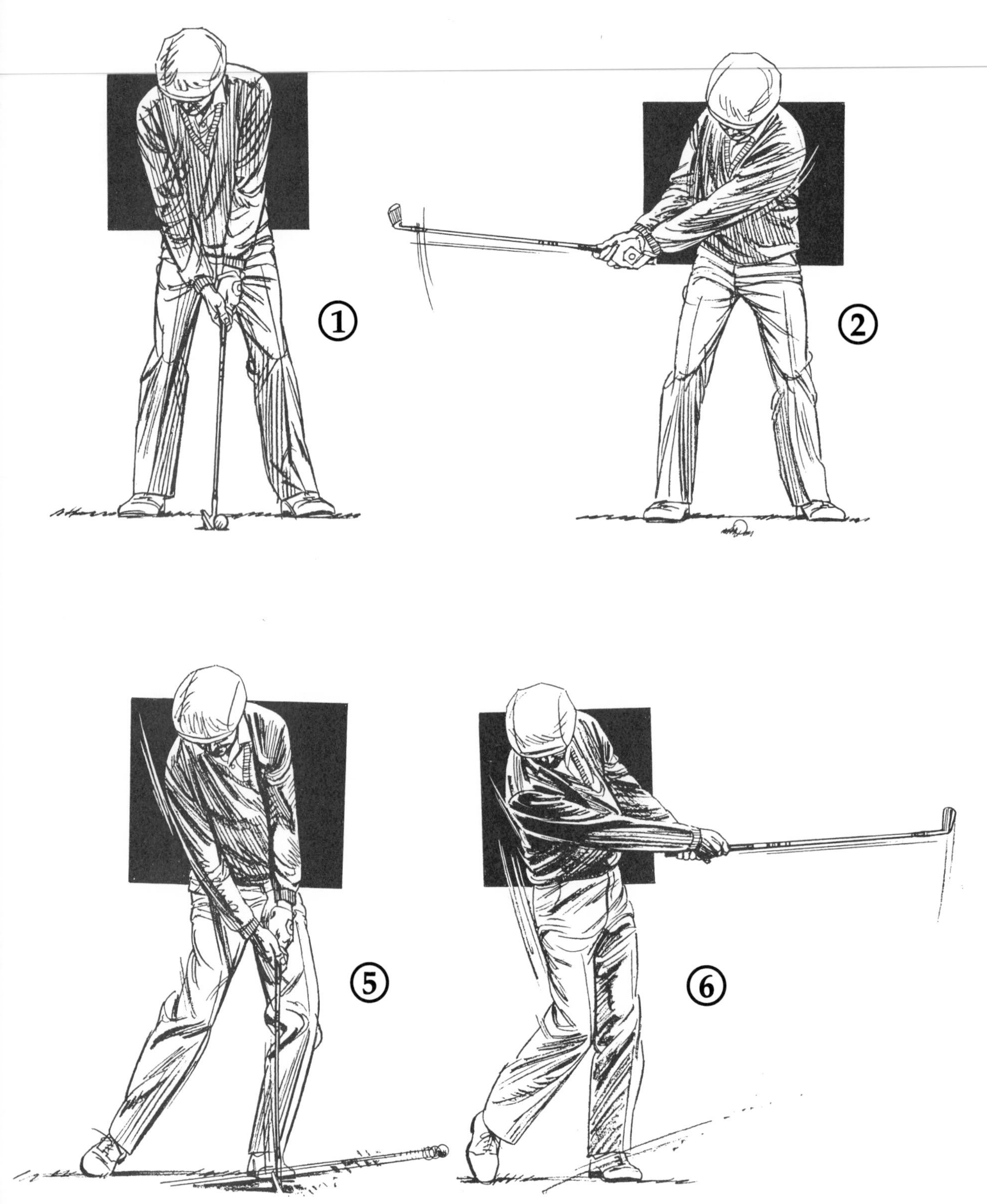

①
②
⑤
⑥

# Your Trunk

It responds, it reacts, it follows. It prepares you to swing.

Even when your spine is set squarely to the line of play, the angle at which it inclines forward to a large extent shapes your swing. A near-vertical spine angle creates a relatively flat swing plane. The farther the spine angle gets from vertical, the more upright the plane of your swing (see illustration).

In the sense that the trunk, through its spine angle, induces or prevents a correct turn and helps shape the

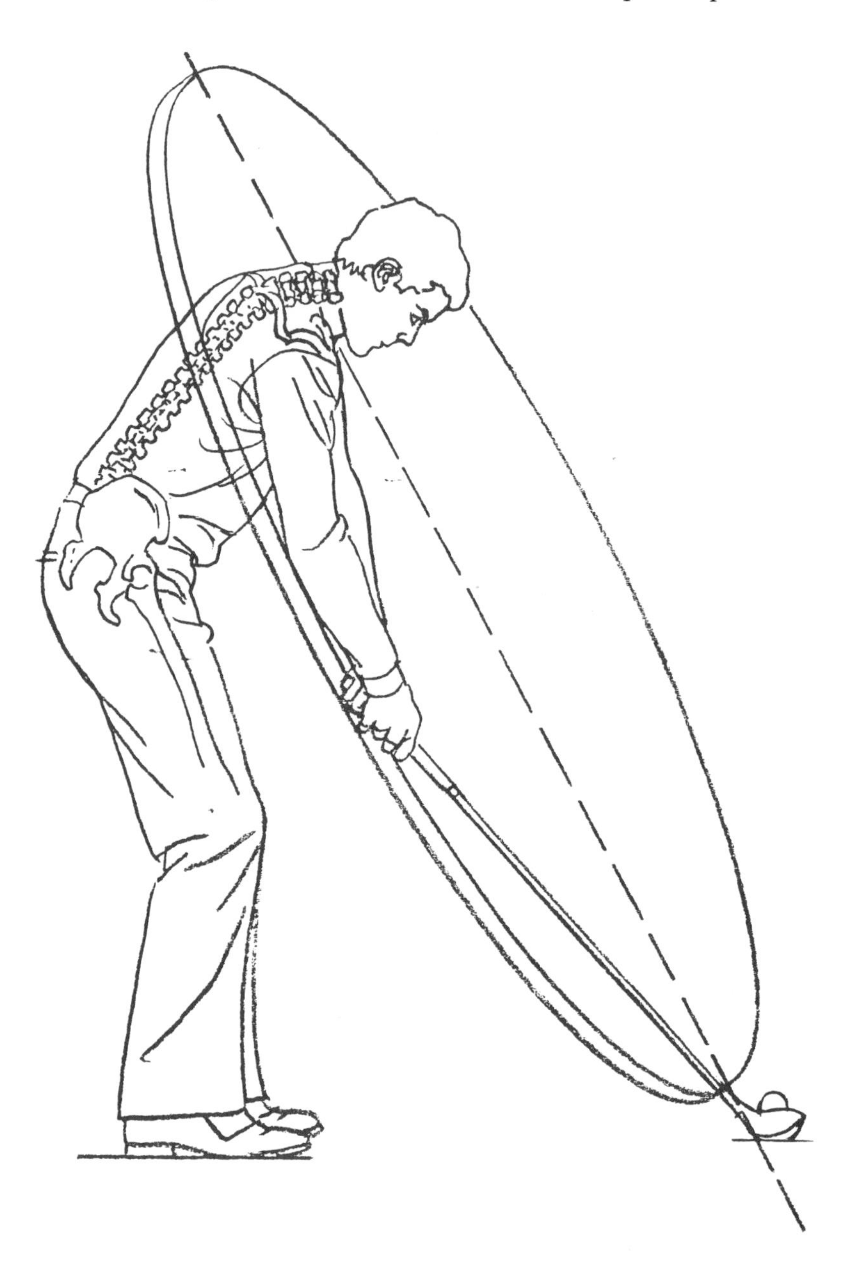

***Spine and plane***
*The more horizontal your spine, the more upright your swing plane. Imagine this golfer leaning forward even more. Notice how the swing plane would become more vertical.*

plane of the swing, it plays a leadership role. But it plays that role only until the swing begins. Once the clubhead is swung back, the trunk's job is to respond—to arms going back, and to both arms and legs coming down.

For many of you the message of this chapter will be, "Quiet down your torso. Quiet down your shoulders. Quiet down your hips." All you have ever heard about the swing is, "Turn, turn, turn," and you've put your torso in charge of the turn. This is a chance to restore it to its proper role. As you study the positions of the trunk during the swing, remember that there is less to do than you thought. Concentrate on the address position and the trunk's important preswing responsibility, and you'll reap large benefits.

## Swing positions

### Address

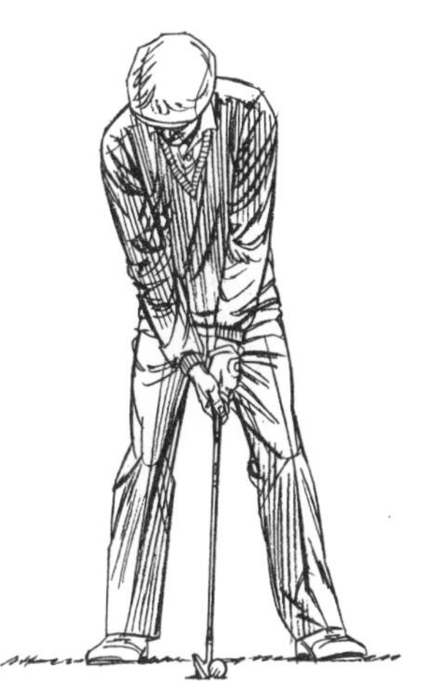

Put this book down for a moment and do this exercise: Face the wall, fold your arms and lean forward until your forehead rests against the wall. Now swing your folded arms from one side to the other under your head, which you are keeping in place. It should be easy to turn to and fro, easy to feel a smooth, natural trunk rotation if your fundamentals are correct. Those fundamentals, which Bob demonstrates beautifully in his address position, are:

1. Spine at a right angle to the line of play, not tilted toward or away from the target.
2. Spine straight, not curved, between head and hips.
3. Shoulders square to the target line.
4. Hips square to the target line.
5. Weight equally distributed between right and left side, in center of feet.

These fundamentals work together. If your spine is not at right angles to the target line, your weight will not be equally distributed between your feet. If your spine is curved or your chin is tucked into your chest, your head will wander when you swing.

The idea is to set your torso at address so that it does not interfere with a proper turn and so that it is ready to respond to the movement of your hands and arms and legs. That should be relatively easy to do for players of standard height—from, say, 5-6 to 6-2. If you are shorter than that or taller than that and you are unsure if your setup posture is correct, you may need a teacher's assistance.

Here's another posture exercise: Holding an iron club just off the ground, take your address while standing on your right leg only. This stance forces you to find the perfect blend of knee flex and hip bend. If it's not right, you will fall off-balance. That's why a tour player often takes his address position by first setting his right leg, feeling his weight on that leg and then swinging his left leg into place. He actually "finds" the proper spine angle while standing on one leg.

## Swinging back

There are two kinds of turns: forced and natural. Bob's turn is a natural turn because it begins with hands and arms swinging the clubhead back and continues with the hips and shoulders and the rest of the torso following. Notice that the hips do not lead; the shoulders do not lead; the rib cage or any other part of the torso does not lead. They respond to the speed and the shape of the swing that the hands and arms create. Bob is fond of saying that a golf swing composed only of hands and arms and no pivot is a lot better than one that begins with a forced pivot. As you swing the club back, remember, your hips, shoulders and trunk have no problem keeping up with the hands and arms if you swing at a reasonable pace. But if you move the massive muscles of the trunk as fast as you can to lead the backswing or downswing—and many amateurs schooled on "pivot" do just that—you will ruin your swing. Your hands and arms will be flung around like a doll in a child's hand.

The angle of Bob's spine shapes his swing by presetting the plane of that swing. With the 5-iron, his swing combines turn and lift about equally. That combination is set at address. With a driver, because the club is longer, he will swing on a flatter plane. With a wedge, the shortest club having the most upright lie, his posture will produce a more up-and-down plane.

The trunk has less distance to travel than the hands and arms do. It is at the center of the swing circle so its arc is shorter. As a result, the trunk can move more slowly than the hands and arms and still reach the "top" of the swing before them. Notice that when Bob's club is halfway back, his trunk, from hips to shoulders, has not turned all that much—it still faces mainly toward the target line. By the time the club is three-fourths of the way to the top, however, it has almost finished turning. The trunk finishes its work and waits for the hands and arms to finish theirs. The shoulders say, in effect, "OK, we have helped you get around, we're just going to take a rest for a second while you complete your backswing and then we're going to start again."

To recapture the feeling of proper shoulder (and trunk) rotation, go back and repeat the Head-to-wall Exercise we suggested earlier. This exercise should not only ingrain the correct rotation, but also give you the feeling of your spine "staying at home" during the swing, allowing your body to turn around it. When your spine stays at home, the chance of your shoulders or hips overpowering the hands and arms is greatly reduced. Shoulders that take over the swing at the top, for example, inevitably twist or tilt the spine on the way down so that the spine cannot "stay at home."

Another way to practice proper trunk motion on the backswing (and later the downswing, too) is to make turns with a long bar. The best kind is an expandable stretch bar

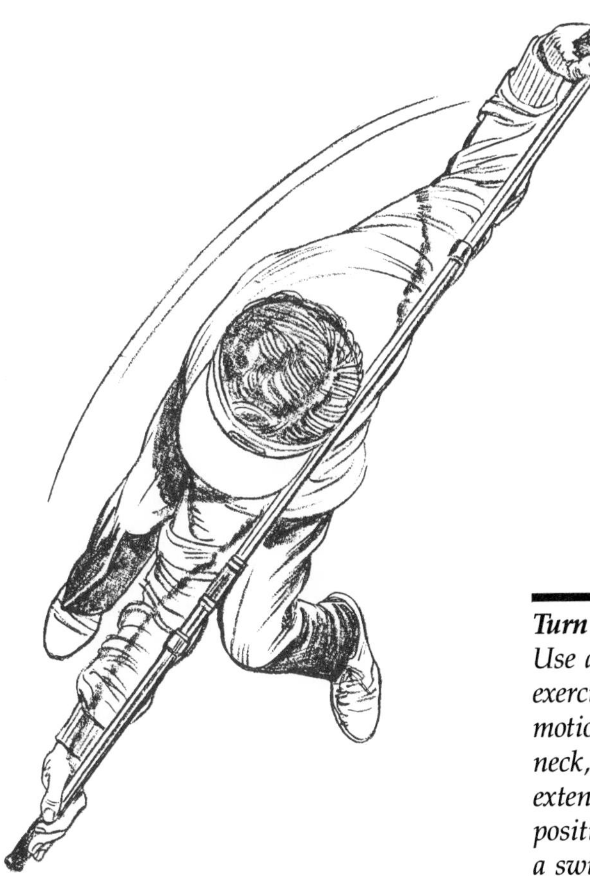

***Turn practice***
*Use a ball retriever or an expandable exercise bar to practice proper trunk motion. Lay the bar over the base of your neck, holding it in place with your arms extended. Take your normal address position and turn as you would during a swing.*

made just for this kind of exercise. The good ones expand to the length of a ball retriever and contract so they are short enough to fit in your golf bag. Lay the fully extended bar across the top of your back at the base of your neck and hold it with your arms fully extended also. Set yourself in your address posture and turn back and forth, first pointing the left end of the bar at a spot on the ground, opposite the center of your body, then the other end of the bar at the same spot. If you miss the spot, you aren't swinging the bar forward on the same plane you swung it back. If you can't reach the spot, you haven't made a big enough turn.

## Swinging down

As Bob begins his downswing, notice how once again the trunk responds to the movement of the hands and arms. The trunk moves more slowly than the hands and arms on the downswing, just as it did on the backswing. Notice how far the club travels before the shoulders make an appreciable movement. The hips are quicker to turn because of the movement of the legs in setting a foundation for the downswing. Still, it's surprising how long the torso remains square to the target line. Even when the hips slide and then begin to turn as the clubhead approaches impact, Bob's shoulders continue to face the line, and remain almost square to the line until after his hands have passed his body. Obviously Bob's torso is responding and reacting to his hands and his arms, not vice versa.

Here's a simple exercise to practice this sequence of movements. With club, but no ball, walk along a line, swinging once every two steps. For right-handers, as you draw the club back, step forward on your left leg. Then swing down and, after completing your downswing, step forward with your right leg. (Left-handers just reverse the process.) This drill also demonstrates that "weight shift" is not something that ought to cause you to jerk your hips around and dominate your hands and arms. After you've mastered this exercise with no ball, tee up five or six balls in a line and walk down the line, hitting them as you go. Do this only when there's no one else on the range.

An even simpler exercise for trunk rotation: Swing a club slowly back and forth, noticing the difference in speed between relatively fast hands and arms and the much slower torso, from hips to shoulders. Gradually add speed, but keep monitoring the difference in the speeds of the two.

## Impact

At impact, Bob's torso faces the line, but his left side, from shoulder to hip, has stretched even more than his right side stretched at the top of the backswing. This isn't something you need to try to do. It's amazing when you think of it: your left hand is going down, your shoulder is going up, you are sliding, you are beginning to turn, and you are stretching. But if a teacher were to tell that to a student, he would have lost him for two days. It would take that long to absorb and then trust and finally quit trying to make that happen. Trust this: This amazing sequence of movements will happen naturally if you allow your torso to respond to the movement of your hands and arms.

***Beneath himself***

*Bob's motion through impact is a perfect example of swinging well "beneath yourself." His spine angle is unaltered. His hands and arms swing past his head and torso as his weight shifts to his left side.*

## Following through

After impact, our theme remains the same: The torso is still reacting to the movement of the hands and arms. The clubhead pulls the arms past the body. The arms pull the shoulders and hips and torso around while the spine stays in almost the same position it occupied at address. Finally, the right shoulder brings the head up.

Bob's swing perfectly demonstrates the same quality of swinging "beneath" oneself that the Head-to-wall Exercise sought to teach. Indeed, you could build an imaginary wall against his head in the down-the-line view, and his head would not have moved from the spot at all. Go back and do the exercise again, now gradually increasing speed until you're swinging almost at the speed you would when you play a shot. Now your "pivot" should be happening automatically, the natural response of your torso to the swinging motion.

## Your Game Plan

**1. Head-to-wall Exercise.** Fold your arms, take your address position and lean forward until your forehead rests against the wall. Now make swings, turning back and forth gently and smoothly enough so that your head does not move.

**2. One-leg Address.** Holding an iron club just off the ground, address the ball while standing on your right leg. Notice the posture you naturally move into in order to keep your balance.

**3. Walk and Swing.** First without a ball, walk forward swinging an iron as you go. As you draw the club back, step forward with your left leg. Then swing down and, after completing your downswing, step forward with your right leg. When it becomes easy to do, tee up six balls and walk down the line, hitting them as you go. Repeat the exercise until you can make solid contact consistently. Be careful. Do this exercise only when the practice area is clear.

**4. Bar Exercise.** Place a ball retriever or an exercise bar across the top of your back at the base of your neck. Take your address position before an imaginary ball and turn right until the left end of the bar points at a spot in front of you above the "ball." Then turn in the other direction until the right end points at the same spot. (Be careful not to strain your back. Don't force the movement. Go as far as you can comfortably.)

5. Hit half-shots with a 7-iron standing first on your left leg only and then on your right. Have the feeling that your head and the top of your spine are remaining relatively still during this exercise.

6. Hit shots with a 7-iron from a right-leg-only stance, stepping into your normal stance as you swing down into the ball.

7. Study the position of Bob's torso during the swing in the sequential drawings on pages 86-87. Get the feel of your torso working the same way as you follow steps A-E on page 11.

# 8 FEELING YOUR HEAD AND EYES

One of the great Buck Adams stories, of which there are many, concerns a visit Ben Crenshaw made to the Country Club of North Carolina when Buck, now a senior tour player, was head pro there. Young Crenshaw had come to play in an amateur event, and Buck walked out with five or six of his members to watch this great college player who was soon to turn pro. The members noticed right away how much Crenshaw moved his head during his swing—he slid it away from the target four or five inches on his backswing, then toward the target four or five inches on his forward swing. After watching Crenshaw for several holes, one of Buck's members said, "What do you think, Buck? What do you think of the way he moves his head?" And Buck said, "I'll tell you one thing. If I had got hold of him when he was 12 or 13 years old, nobody would know his name now."

What Buck meant, of course, was that he and most other teachers would have "fixed" that moving head and, arguably, fouled up Ben Crenshaw for life. Ben was proving that no matter what the instruction books said about "keeping your head down," he could play pretty well with quite a lot of head movement. Indeed, when Ben went to his own teacher, the great Harvey Penick, after someone did try to fix that head, Harvey said, "Don't change it, Ben. That is not the way you play."

That may strike you as an odd story with which to begin our chapter on Head and Eyes, but it makes the point: At least as much damage is done to the average amateur's swing in the name of keeping his head still (or down) as is done by his moving it. Like so many other desirable positions in golf, a still head is a result, not a cause.

We want you to swing with a steady head—or more precisely, with a steady top-of-the-spine. We hope to have you swinging with a steady head by the time you finish your work with this chapter, but we hope it will be the byproduct of some other good habits—and not because you have buried your head in your chest and used all the tension in your neck and back muscles to keep it there. We don't want you to *try* to keep it down.

Part of your achieving proper head movement will depend on how you use your eyes, during and especially before your swing. We'll help you work on that, also.

Before we look at the way Bob uses his head and eyes during the swing, a few incontrovertible facts: There is head movement during the swing. In their landmark book, *The Search for the Perfect Swing,* Alastair Cochran and John Stobbs proved so by placing an electrode on the head of a model golfer and filming that golfer in the dark. During the swing the marker moved in a tiny circle. It moved back an inch or two, down an inch or two, forward an inch or two and up an inch or two, finishing in almost the same posi-

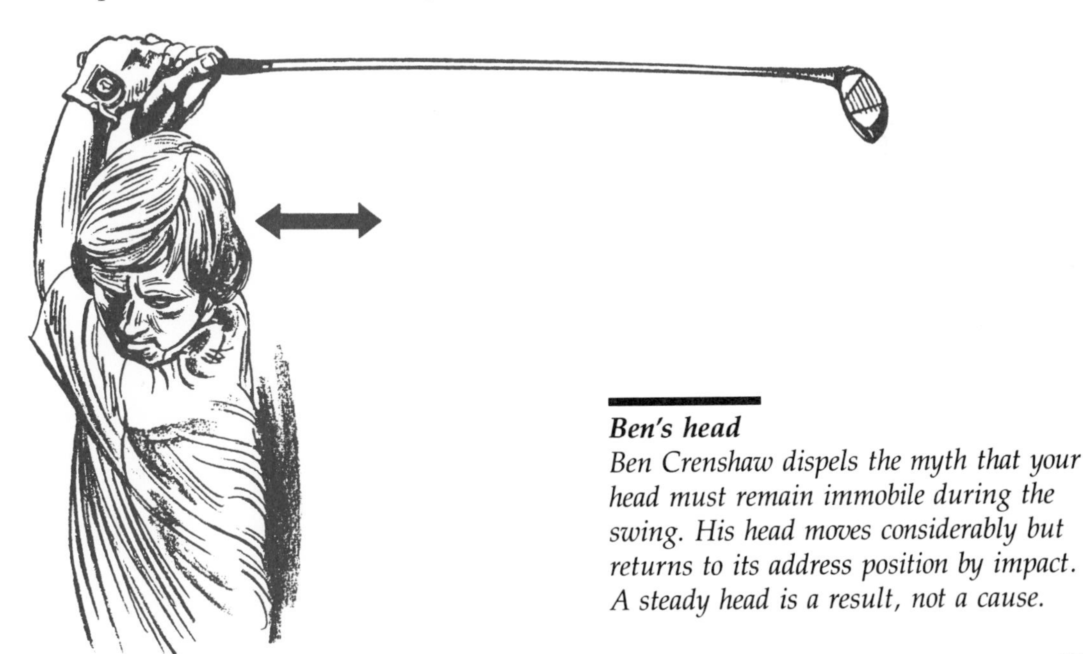

***Ben's head***
*Ben Crenshaw dispels the myth that your head must remain immobile during the swing. His head moves considerably but returns to its address position by impact. A steady head is a result, not a cause.*

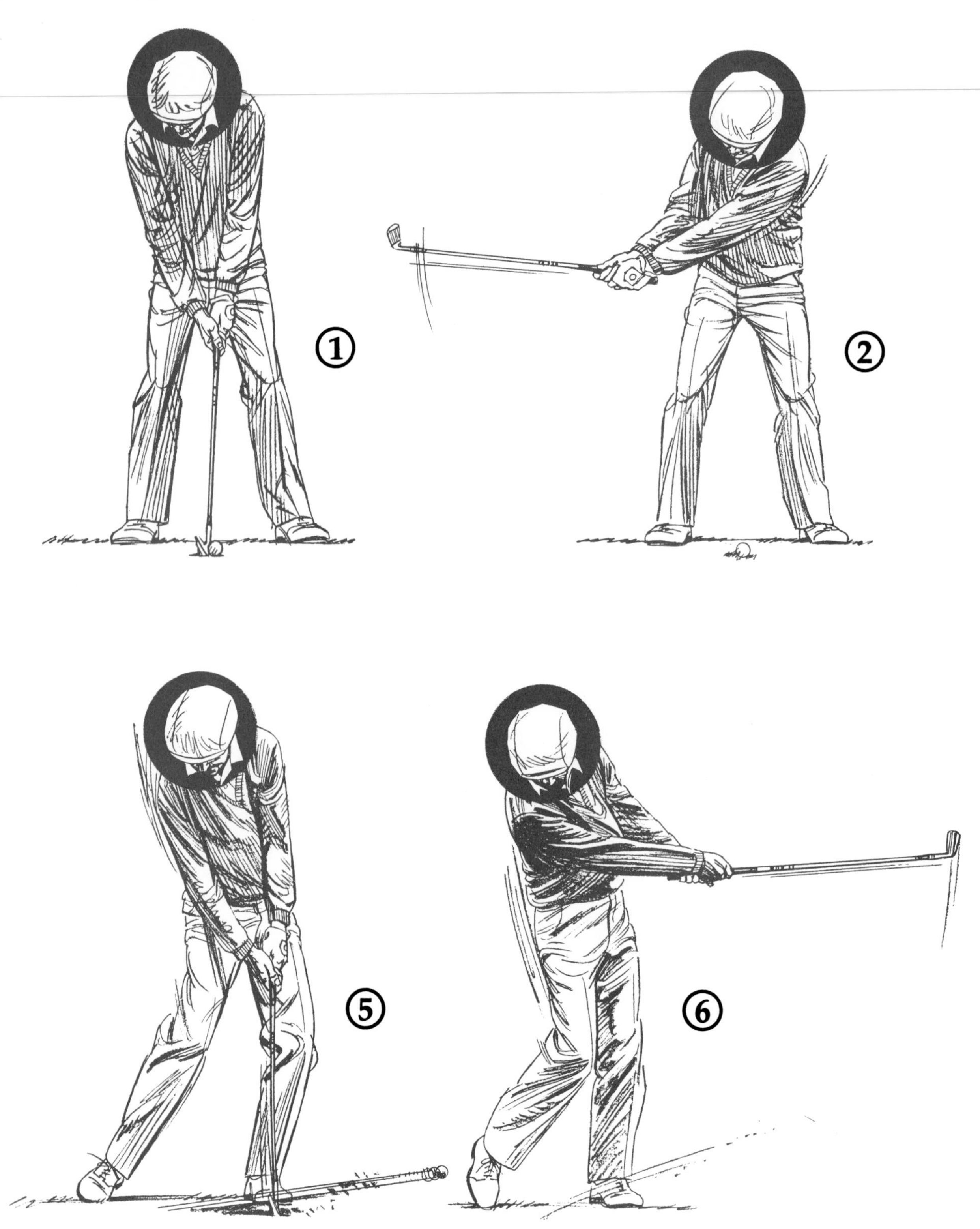
①
②
⑤
⑥

# Your Head and Eyes

## The keys to a centered, accurate golf swing.

tion as it began. Biomechanics expert Dr. Ralph Mann has done similar research recently with computers and high-speed cameras. His verdict is identical: minimal movement, but movement.

So that's what you're aiming for—not an immobile head, but a steady one, a quiet one. A quiet head is the sign of a swinger—as opposed to a hitter—because the more you swing the club and the more centrifugal force that the swinging club creates, the stiller and quieter the center of that force wants to be. A hitter of the ball, on the other hand, tends to move his head—right on the backswing, left on the forward swing—to increase leverage. You want to be a swinger.

One of the best drills for achieving "quietness" is the Right Foot, Left Toe Exercise (see illustration). Do it now. Stand on your right foot with your left toe resting on a spot behind you, about the same distance toward the target from

***Right foot, left toe***
*To experience swinging around a quiet head, make hip-to-hip swings standing on your right foot with your left foot placed on its toe just behind you. Don't try to keep your head in place. It will happen naturally.*

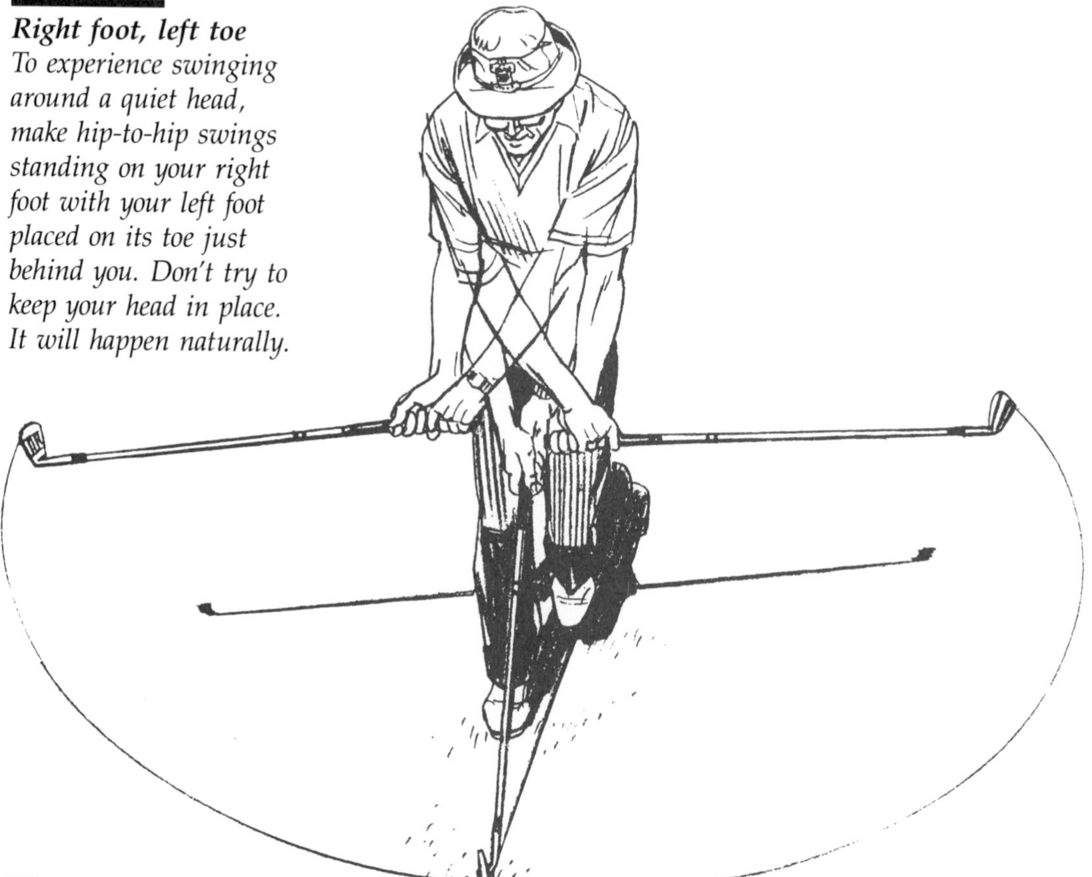

your right foot as it would be when you take your stance. (The ball should be opposite your right foot.) Swing the club back and forth. You'll notice that if your head begins to move, you will lose your balance. You can't stay in balance and do this exercise without the "quiet" head we are talking about. But that stillness is a result of swinging naturally and in balance. Now try keeping your head absolutely still while you swing. Chances are, that effort to keep your head still only botches things up. Remember, the "quiet" head is a result, not a cause. Later, hit some balls doing the Right Foot, Left Toe Exercise, monitoring your head movement. Don't try to keep it in place. Just notice how your head does or does not move and how its movement relates to your shot.

*Forcing your head down or forcing your head to be still doesn't work because it creates tension.* Neck muscles are one place where players tend to get very tight and forcing your head to stay in one place will tense those muscles every time. Players advised to keep their heads still do it by tightening the large muscles that run from the neck down to the shoulders. The result is not only a tight neck but tense shoulders, too, and, ultimately, a restricted turn. You may succeed in keeping your head down, but you'll be unable to get the clubhead swinging because you can't turn your body. Test this for yourself with another exercise: Fold your arms and swing back and forth while looking at a spot between your feet. Make sure you're swinging freely enough so that you can see your feet at the top of your "swing." Now do the exercise while forcing your head to stay absolutely, rigidly still. How does that affect your turn? What does it do to your balance?

***Chin to chest***
*Forcing your chin into your chest in an effort to keep it still will only increase tension and prevent a free arm swing.*

Inevitably, when a golfer attempts to "keep his head down" he pushes it into his chest and that creates yet another obstacle to a free turn, as we explained in the last chapter. He can't get his shoulders to turn without moving his head and since he's committed to keeping his head in place, he has little turn. Try this instead: Imagine that your head is "floating" above your feet and above the ball and that you are swinging beneath it.

In order to do that, you'll need space between your chin and your chest. Our colleague, Jim Flick, suggests you measure the distance this way: Form a 90-degree angle with your right thumb and index finger the way you would if you

**_Chin Check_**
*To establish proper head and chin position at address, make a "gun" with your right hand, then point the thumb into your sternum and your index finger under your chin.*

made a "gun" with your hand. Now point the gun straight up in the air, with the thumb touching your sternum and the tip of your finger under your chin (see illustration). That's about how much space you need between chin and chest to achieve a "floating" head. Davis says he feels almost as though his head is disconnected, watching his body move freely underneath it, as he swings.

There are two images, then, to remember as you study the drawings of Bob's swing: a "quiet" head and a "floating" head. Notice how he embodies them.

A note about your eyes. You'll find it easier to achieve this sense of suspension and quietness if you set your eyes correctly at address. Setting them square to the line of play, for example, makes swinging beneath your head simpler. Setting them off line causes you to swing off-center and, as a result, tug your head in one direction or another. What's more, your eyes are your preswing check on whether you're aligned correctly—if you know how to use them. We'll show you in a moment. Finally, your eyes—or your "inner" eyes—help you visualize shots before you make them. "Seeing" the perfect shot before swinging makes it likelier you'll see it afterward.

## Head position during address

Bob cocks his head to the right slightly at address. (Jack Nicklaus does the same thing.) That makes him feel that his shoulder turn will be unrestricted and that he'll stay behind the ball. What's important is that once Bob gets his head set there, it stays there. Look at his position at impact—it's almost identical to his address position. His head has remained steady.

Does Bob look in the least bit tense at address? Not at all. Like the "gun position" described above, Bob's head is well above his chest. His neck shows no signs of rigidness or holding. He has given his lower body and shoulders plenty of room to swing "beneath" his head, but if that shoulder turn should cause the head to move, you don't get the feeling here that the neck and head will fight it. His head hangs between his feet, almost directly over his hands. His eyes are focused on the ball. He is in perfect position to swing around the "quiet" and "suspended" head we spoke of earlier.

Although the sequence drawings cannot show it, Bob's eye movements are important during address, too. Good players use their eyes two ways here: They check alignment and they focus on the target. It's important that both are done carefully.

Here are two tips on checking your alignment: First, make a target line with clubs, rope or ribbon. Then, once you've taken your stance, check your body position vis-à-vis the target line by matching that line to your eye line. You shouldn't have to tilt your head to have both eyes looking directly at the target line when you look down at the ball. If you wear glasses, you can check that alignment by placing a piece of thread or dental floss across the lenses. (If you don't wear glasses, use a nonprescription pair.) The thread should seem to cover the target line as you address the ball.

Another alignment check, this one from our Golf Digest Schools colleague Jack Lumpkin: After you've addressed the ball, look at your target and back at the ball before you hit. If done correctly, this will tell you if you are misaligned. The trick is to move only your head and eyes as you check the target. Watch a pro and you will see him carefully rotate his head from the ball to the target. He won't raise his head

***Your "window"***
*To check your aim, rotate your head slowly toward the target without moving your shoulders. Learn to look into the same "window" each time. You aren't looking for the target. You're looking through the window to see if the target is there. If not, realign.*

or move his neck. He won't look over his shoulder. He wants to "discover" the target in his vision, not turn his head looking for the target. He trusts that the target will be in the "window" he looks through after he rotates his head (see previous illustration). If it's not, he knows he's misaligned and he sets up again. Many poorer players, however, make any head, neck or shoulder movement necessary to find the target. As a consequence they don't know if they are correctly aligned.

That look has another purpose, too. It's your chance to focus on the one and only object of this swing: your target. Get into it! Take a leisurely, lingering look, giving yourself plenty of time to pick up details about the green or fairway at which you're aiming so that you'll have no doubt, as you're swinging, where you want the ball to go. Too many players are so quick with those eye movements they don't have a chance to get the information they need to really zero in on the target. You have to give your eyes time to focus. The farther away the target, the longer that takes. There are those who argue that you can play this game while being self- or swing-oriented rather than target-oriented. We doubt it. After playing with and watching some of the game's great players, we believe target awareness is essential. Stephen King has yet to write a book that could scare

***Ben's eyes***

*Hogan's gaze was steely because his eyes were so intent on the target. They devoured it. Use your eyes to absorb course and wind conditions. Then zero in on the target like Ben did.*

you as much as looking into Ben Hogan's eyes as he was about to drive a ball into the center of the fairway or knock an iron shot stiff. Billy Casper has some of the meanest eyes ever seen when he was looking at the hole. We joked, at the time, that some players could "hate" it into the hole. Casper was like that when he was putting. He had three things on his mind: target, target, target. That look you make at your target before you swing should devour your target, too.

## Swinging back

We wish we could show you the rest of this swing sequence on videotape. As apparent as the steadiness of Bob's head and eyes are in these drawings, the grace and ease with which he maintains the positions would bowl you over on videotape. But the message is, a steady head isn't forced to be steady; it wants to be steady. Like the head of a dancer whose body cha-chas beneath him, a golfer's head is in the center of the action. The faster the clubhead whirls down and around him, the more his head wants to steady that movement. The backswing is preparation for that coming "storm." The head is comfortable, the eyes are fixed on the ball, the neck muscles are reasonably relaxed. By the top of the backswing, the shoulder has moved past the chin, the weight has shifted from one side to the other, the arms have rotated and lifted, but the head remains centered, steady, suspended, the fixed point around which the swing arc is created.

To feel the clubhead whirling around and steadying that "center," swing an iron club with your left arm only, holding your left forearm with your right hand, thumb pointed up. Make nice easy swings at first. Then graduate to hitting teed balls with a 7- or 8-iron.

## At impact

Compare the head positions at address and at impact. They are almost identical. If there has been movement it is the tiny circular movement that the researchers talk about. There is no dipping of the head here—a common fault among amateurs. There is also no sliding of the head left. Bob's eyes are on the ball. His "inner" eyes are on the target. He has kept his head and his swing center steady—level and unsliding—so that the club can make a smooth, circular swing around them. He has no interest in following the ball at this point. His head and eyes have a different job: to be the fulcrum around which his club swings. In a split second Bob's hands and arms will whisk past his eyes. Bob's head will not move until his right shoulder, pulled by the force of the arms and hands (which in turn are pulled by the clubhead), pushes his chin up. If your head remains steady you'll have the feeling of hips, shoulders, arms and hands all rotating into the ball around that unchanging swing center.

## Following through

As the right shoulder forces your head up, what are you looking for? The ball? That's the natural response, but a good habit to get into is to look immediately at your target and then let your eyes drift back to the ball if it's not there already. (This is great for putting.) This will break you of the habit of "chasing" the ball with your head and eyes. It will also encourage you to stay engrossed in the target.

Notice how long it takes for Bob's head to come up. His clubshaft is well past parallel on the left side of his body before his head has moved even two inches. That steady head is the byproduct of his staying square to the target line as long as he does. His image of swinging "beneath his head" helps him to do that.

To practice "staying home", that is, swinging under and past that quiet, suspended head, return to the Swish Exercise we did in Chapter 4. Place a business card on the carpet, or a tee far into the ground, and swing a short iron back and forth over the spot, attempting to hit the spot both ways while keeping the swing continuous. Notice the direct relationship between a steady head and hitting the spot.

## Your Game Plan

### ☐☐Head

1. Study the positioning of the head at address. Notice how little it changes during the swing (see pages 98-99).

**2. Thumb-forefinger Check.** Check the space between your chin and your chest by pointing at your chin with your right forefinger while pushing your thumb into your chest. Make a few iron swings—no ball—concentrating on chin placement.

**3. Right Foot, Left Toe Drill.** Take your address position, and with the ball opposite your right foot, move your left foot away from the target line and rest it on its toes. Make swings from this position, first without a ball and then while hitting three-quarter 7-, 8- and 9-iron shots. This drill teaches you to swing in balance. Feel your swing happening around and below your head.

**4. Swish Exercise.** Pick a spot on the carpet or place a tee well into the ground, and swing a club back and forth at the spot. Swing slowly enough so that you know you are hitting the spot in both directions. The steadier your head is, the easier that will be.

### ☐☐Eyes

**1. Glasses Check.** Mark a target line with clubs, rope, ribbon, etc. Attach a rubber band to your glasses so that the band describes a horizontal line across the lenses. Take your stance with an iron club, adjusting your head and eyes until the band appears to lie on the target line. Make some swings without a ball. When you get to the range, hit easy 8-irons with the band in place. Notice how this new position feels.

**2. "Window" Check.** On the range, establish a target and target line. Address a ball with an iron club and check your alignment by rotating your head—move nothing else, not shoulders, not arms—90 degrees to your left. Is the target in the "window" of what you now see? If not, realign and check it again.

**3. Target Search.** Hit 7- or 8-irons to a specific target on the range. As you strike the ball and your shoulder brings your head up, look first at your target and then move back until you find the ball. Repeat this exercise until finding the target first is second nature.

▽ ▽ ▽ ▽ ▽ ▽ ▽ ▽ ▽ ▽

# 9
# PUTTING IT TOGETHER

It's time to blend new and old into a swing that's entirely yours, entirely comfortable, and most of all, durable. It's time to put it together.

"Putting it together" means graduating from learning to playing. It means melding the movements of individual body parts into a swing. It means moving from a feeling of, say, hands, to a feeling of the swing as a whole. And the swing, remember, is a swing of the clubhead.

We began with the movement of the clubhead and proceeded to how individual body parts contribute to swinging the club. Now we return to the club and concentrate on *the club moving the ball.* Remember, the ball understands only one thing: what the clubface does to it. We can feel anything we like but if we have not delivered the clubface squarely to the ball at the proper angle of approach, at the proper speed on the proper path, our feeling is for nought.

So putting it together ultimately requires what Bob calls the three "Ps"—Practice, Perseverance and Patience.

To match self-awareness to club and swing awareness, and ultimately to ball flight and target awareness, you'll need to master *rhythm, balance* and *pace.* You'll have to work on *plane* and *path.* And that takes *practice.* As a result, we'll start by spending a lot of time on how to practice.

Mention the word practice to some players and you've lost them. They love to study the swing and they love to play, but, please, no range balls. If you're a member of the

***The first "P"***
*Practice is the first of Bob's three "Ps"—Perseverance and Patience are next.*

no-practice club, give us a chance to explain how practice can and should be an engaging adjunct to your play, not a purgatorial sentence imposed for high scores.

## Practice guidelines

Many players decide practice is drudgery—and derive little benefit from it—because they don't adhere to The Four Great Love/Toski Guidelines for All Practice Sessions:

1. Hit more good shots than bad. That means: Use a tee to make it easier, make easy swings with lofted clubs and do whatever else you need to hit most of your shots solidly.
2. Challenge yourself. As soon as you're hitting more good shots than bad, make it harder. Remove the tee, make a faster swing, use more club. But be willing to back off immediately when you've begun hitting more bad shots so that you can regain your success.

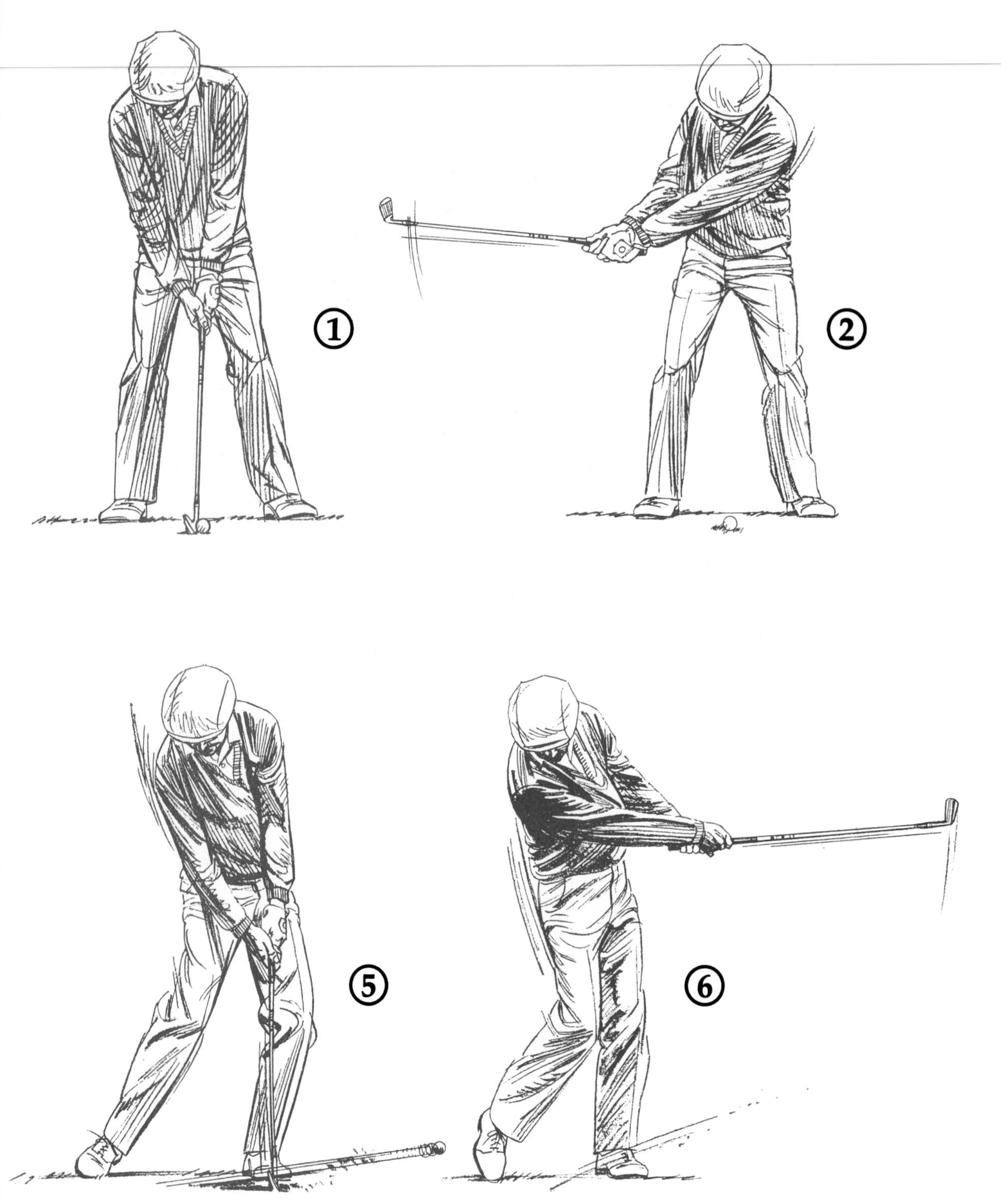
①
②
⑤
⑥

# Putting It Together

## There's no way around it: Perfecting your new swing requires practice and patience.

3. Make more practice swings than shots. It's hard to discipline yourself to do this, but swings without a ball help you master swing changes quickly.
4. Always work at a practice "station," assuring yourself proper alignment and ball position.

Actually, the four work together. Although you ought to challenge yourself during a practice session by working on your weaknesses and not just your strengths, don't walk to the range after a day of duck-hooking your driver and duck-hook yourself into a dither. Start with a club you hit well that day—your 7-iron, say—and make some shots you like. Then try to carry that swing over to the driver. If you hit a bunch of bad ones in a row, go back and hit good shots with a club in which you have confidence. Don't let the foozles overtake you.

That won't happen if you observe guideline No. 3. Taking the time to make a rehearsal swing that is really a rehearsal of the shot you want to make will keep you from mindlessly beating balls. It will help you find the fault that's causing the problem (it's much easier to feel a flaw when there's not a ball to worry about) and it will establish a relaxed, leisurely pace for your practice.

And to evaluate whether a shot is good or bad, you need a practice station. That means laying down a club to establish your target line; placing a club or a marker at right angles to assure proper ball position; and painting in a path line so that you can see where your club is approaching the ball.

We know laying down clubs and using spray paint may be embarrassing. But that's part of what it takes to become a proficient player. Tom Kite, at one of our Golf Digest outings, was asked by an amateur how he felt about drills and practice aids. The student said he would be embarrassed to use them on his club range. "What about me?" Tom replied. "I walk onto a tournament practice range and maybe I have Tom Watson on one side of me and Jack Nicklaus on the other. I'm making half swings, hitting teed balls with a 7-iron. That's embarrassing, too." "Then why do you keep doing it?" asked the amateur. "Because," said Kite, "I like winning better than losing." At the 1986 World Series of Golf, in a field composed entirely of tournament winners, Kite could be seen wearing one of the "flying elbow" harnesses Golf Digest Schools instructor Peter

***Kite's drills***
*Tom Kite is willing to do sometimes embarrassing drills—like hitting irons off a tee—for one reason: They pay off!*

Kostis had given him. Embarrassing? You bet. But Kite and players like him are willing to do whatever it takes to become as good as they are. We urge you to use whatever drills or practice aids it takes to feel your swing. Those moments of embarrassment will pay off in accomplishments later.

## Feeling the whole swing

As you begin putting your swing together, you have four goals. First, squaring the clubface at impact, meaning that the leading edge runs roughly perpendicular to the target line at impact and sends the ball directly toward the target. Second, moving the clubhead into the ball on the correct path, generally inside to along the target line to inside but varying slightly depending on the club. Third, striking the ball with the right angle of approach (descending, ascending, or "sweeping"), which is a function of both path and plane (more later). Fourth, swinging at the proper speed.

## Address

Some general comments on setup. We spoke a great deal about proper posture in the Trunk, and Head and Eyes Chapters. The ideal posture is what we called the "linebacker" posture: Weight on the balls of the feet, feet spread hip-width, knees flexed, buttocks raised slightly, spine straight, head forward between the feet. One trick to establishing this "athletic ready" posture is to hold the club with your left hand only as you address the ball. After you have the club square to the line behind the ball and your feet set squarely to the line, bring your right hand around and grip the club (see illustration). You'll find your posture is already very close to the ideal.

***Right hand***
*Once your posture is set, aim the club with your left hand and bring your right hand "quietly" around without disturbing your setup.*

A note on ball position. You've heard some instructors say play the ball off the left heel for every shot. You've heard some say play the ball off the left heel for the driver and move it steadily back until it's near the right foot for pitch shots. It's our feeling that the range of ball position is neither as unchanging as the first advice nor as variable as the second. Start with the ball in the middle of your stance and move it a total of three or four golf balls forward as you go from your wedge to your driver. Play your short irons in the position farthest back, your wood clubs in the position farthest forward. Experiment to find the right position for the clubs in the middle. If the ball is too far forward—and many amateurs play it too far forward encouraging a slice—the clubhead is already moving upward and left when it reaches the ball. If the ball is too far back, the clubhead's approach is steeply downward and to the right as it reaches the ball. Experiment with the four-ball model to find the right ball position for each of your clubs.

## Squaring the clubface

Like the baseball hitter who plays a game of pepper before stepping into the batting cage or the soccer team that kicks a ball in a circle before taking the field, start small as you put your swing together. Begin by swinging a 7-iron from hip to hip. After you're confident that the clubface is meeting the ball squarely, straight down the target line, increase the length of your swings to shoulder to shoulder. When you're consistently hitting your target, move on to full swings, concentrating still on the movement of the clubhead, but being aware of making a smooth, rhythmic swing.

Proceed from hip-to-hip to full swing only when you're hitting more good shots than bad. If you run into a spell of dubs, go back from full swing to shoulder-to-shoulder or hip-to-hip swings to establish control. But if you hit three straight good ones with the shorter swing, get back on the ladder. The idea is to make a full swing with the same confidence you had with the hip-to-hip swing.

## Feeling the path

It's Davis' humble belief that you'll never master path until you master spray paint. He was one of the great paint users of all time—still is—and we hope you will be, too. There is no easier way, once you've mastered solid, square contact, to master path than by painting it on the ground (see illustration). Your path line should curve back and inward from the ball. It will vary slightly with the lie of the club you're hitting. What's important is having an aid to help you get the club started back properly and a line with which to monitor your downswing so that you know the club is coming from the inside to along the target line. Better even than a single line is a double "highway" line the width of your clubface, through which you swing the club. Some players think they can monitor path without a line like this. Trust us. Seeing and feeling path are twice as good as trying to feel it only. Ask your professional to help you determine the proper path for you. Then paint your "teacher" on the ground.

***Dr. Spray***
*Mark your intended swing path with spray paint to make checking your progress easier. It's like having a teacher on the ground.*

Work from hip-to-hip swings to full swing, this time concentrating only on path. In each category, start with slow-motion swings, making sure you are swinging the club back and through along the proper path. Don't worry too much about ball flight at this point. Get the path down and then, as you increase speed, work on shot result. If in establishing path you have trouble squaring the clubface or making solid contact, backtrack to shorter shots as you did above.

## The planest truth

You've probably heard of Ben Hogan's pane of glass and, more recently, of the swing-plane machines that put you at the center of a giant dinner plate and get you sliding the club across the surface to master swing plane.

Both those planes have their problems. We'd rather borrow a simpler model from another Hogan, instructor Chuck Hogan, who has made his name of late as a "mental side" expert, but who is a former PGA club pro, too. Hogan's model is a foolproof way to understand plane. It also accounts for changes in plane from one club to the next.

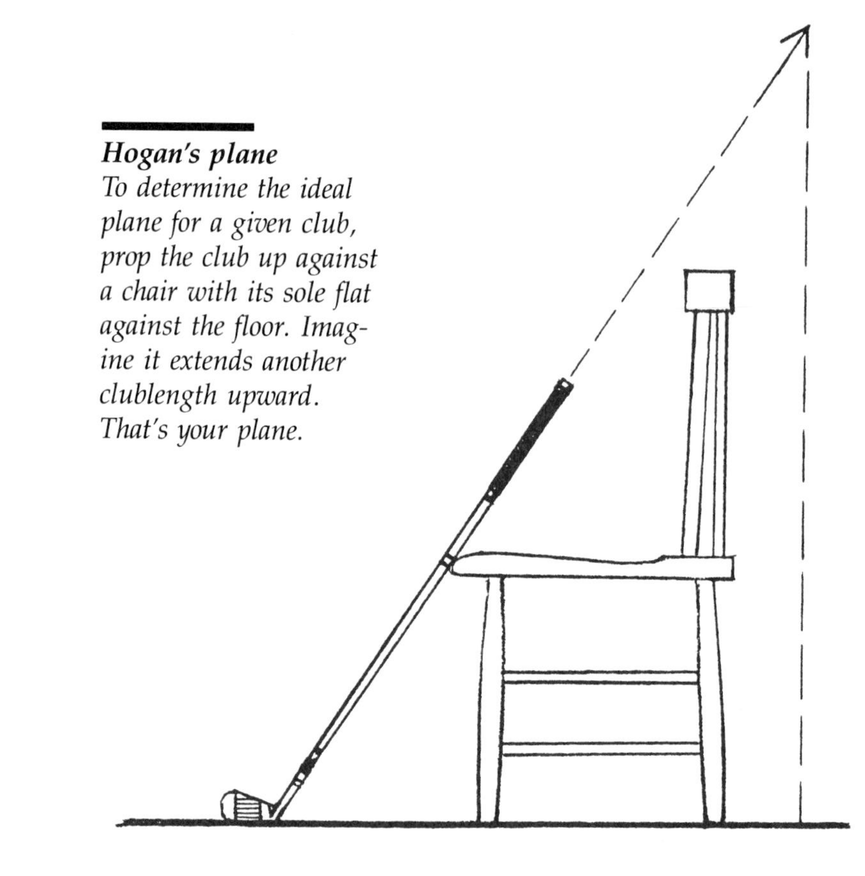

***Hogan's plane***
*To determine the ideal plane for a given club, prop the club up against a chair with its sole flat against the floor. Imagine it extends another clublength upward. That's your plane.*

***Irwin's flume***
*Two-time U.S. Open champion Hale Irwin imagines his club swinging down along a flume. Create your own imaginary device to make swinging on-plane easier.*

Prop a 7-iron against a chair. Make sure the sole of the club sits flat along the floor (see illustration opposite). Walk out along the club's imaginary target line. Turn around and look back at it. That's your swing plane with a 7-iron. At impact, your clubshaft must lie along or under that shaft at address. As you practice hip-to-hip and then shoulder-to-shoulder and finally full swings, concentrate on swinging the club into the ball under or along the plane. Try different clubs. Hit a 9-iron and then a 7- and a 5- and notice how the plane changes. The longer the club—driver being the longest, wedge the shortest—the flatter the plane. Hogan's method is simple because it is scientific. The 7-iron was designed to swing on the plane its shaft describes at address. Swinging it above the plane will force you to approach the ball from outside the target line. Swinging it below the plane still allows an inside-out path.

As you swing and test this principle with different clubs, create an image of your own plane. Hale Irwin thinks of his shaft sliding through a flume as it approaches the ball. One pro who has worked with Chuck Hogan imagines a laser detector lying along the plane so that if the shaft should approach the ball from above the plane an alarm goes off. Create your own image. Make it a cement plane or an electronic plane or a glass plane—whatever makes it easiest for you to feel the proper plane.

Remember, the important plane is the downswing plane. It determines the angle at which the shaft approaches the ball at impact. But swinging the club back along or under the plane makes finding that correct downswing path much easier.

## Feeling your optimum speed

The final ingredient after proper path, plane and solid contact is pace: your maximum, most effective swing speed. We aren't proponents of swinging slowly. On the contrary we want you to swing the clubhead as fast as you can while maintaining control. That is, we want you to swing the club as fast as you can (1) if you stay in balance and (2) if you maintain accuracy.

Pretty big "ifs" you're probably saying to yourself. But they needn't be. We've presented you with a dozen exercises to help you find that swing speed in other parts of the book. Swinging two clubs at once. Swinging on one leg. Swinging with your eyes closed. Swinging while calling out your grip pressure and trying to keep it constant. Swinging one arm only.

Choose one or two of the drills that most appealed to you and work with them now to generate a pace you can live with. As with path and plane, work up from mini to full swings. Backtrack from middle irons to short irons when necessary.

## Intention and attention

In order to make this new swing truly your own, we urge you to practice with a specific INTENTION for every swing and with maximum ATTENTION to make it happen. Swing changes don't happen overnight. Habits don't break because we want them to. The more you hit each shot with a specific intention and the more attentive you are to achieving that goal on each shot, the faster your progress will be. If, for example, your intention is to make swings at half speed, ask yourself after each shot: "Did I swing at half speed? How did the swing motion feel?" What's more, you'll ingrain fastest what you do with most repetition. Some psychologists suggest that it takes three weeks, 21 consecutive days, to establish a habit. As you work on particular elements of your swing—feeling the hands square the club at impact for example—use that model. Hit 60 shots a day for 21 days—or as many of those 21 days as possible—and concentrate on that feeling. Then move on to a new specific objective. Commit yourself to that kind of consistent effort, and you will "put it together" very quickly.

## Mind games help, too

In the next chapter we will talk about taking your new swing onto the course. But the transition from practice to play begins both on the range and at home. At the end of each practice session, play a few imaginary holes. Decide on a course you know, start on the first hole and play nine holes. Hit your tee shot, decide how it ended up and choose a club for your approach shot. If you still have a pitch to reach the green hit a pitch shot. Then give yourself two putts and move on to the next hole. You create the day's pin placements. You decide what the wind's doing. You say whether it's soggy or dry. It's amazing how realistic this kind of practice becomes. If you bring your full intention and attention to it, those hazards and out-of-bounds get very foreboding. But you learn to deal with the nervousness they generate on the practice range—not out on the course where it will cost you. Make it real, and you'll have a sense of déjà vu on the course. You'll make the good shot because you've made it before.

Mental practice at home is just as helpful if you make it real. Sit in a quiet room, close the door, turn off the phone and play a round of golf. Make it a match against someone you really would like to beat. Get into it. What is the lie of your shot like? Is that monarch butterfly flashing around it? What will the speck of mud do to the ball flight? Feel your palms getting clammy as you step up to a tight driving hole. Imagine smooth, balanced swings and sure-handed putts. Let yourself celebrate these great shots and be disappointed when the bounces don't go your way. Let it be just as real as a dream or nightmare. Really let go and you'll break scoring barriers you've been struggling with for years.

## Your Game Plan

### ☐☐Setup

**Ball-position Exercise.** Place four balls adjacent to one another along a line parallel to the target line as markers. Take a stance so that the ball farthest back is directly under your sternum. Beginning with the wedge, hit 10 or 20 shots from that ball position. Then move up a ball and hit 7-irons. Move up another ball and hit 5-irons. Finally, hit 3-woods opposite the ball farthest forward. Notice how the club's angle of approach changes with very little movement of the ball in your stance.

### ☐☐Squaring the Clubface

**Graduation Drill.** Using your knowledge of ball position, hit hip-to-hip shots, then shoulder-to-shoulder shots and finally full-swing shots, concentrating solely on delivering the clubface squarely to the ball. Use a 7-iron at first, and don't move to the next largest swing until you are making solid contact with the last. Backtrack when you need to keep hitting more good shots than poor ones.

### ☐☐Finding the Path

**Paint-a-path Exercise.** Spray-paint a target line, then spray-paint a "path" line, curving inward off the target line. Make shoulder-to-shoulder swings so that your takeaway and downswing approximate the painted path. Move on to longer clubs and notice how the natural path moves more inward as the club gets longer.

### ☐☐Swinging on Plane

**1. Chuck Hogan's Plane.** Ask a friend to take his stance with a 9-iron, making sure the club's sole rests squarely on the ground. Walk out along the club's target line, turn around and look at it. Create an imaginary plane from the blade, along the shaft, through your friend's body a clublength on the other side of him. Then ask him to switch to a 7-iron, a 5-iron, a 3-iron and finally a driver. Notice how the imaginary plane changes. Now, you hold the club and let him do the imagining.

**2. Plane Practice.** Hit three-quarter shots with a 9-iron, concentrating solely on delivering the club to the ball so that the shaft lies on or below the plane it established at address. As you gain confidence that your plane is correct, graduate to 7-, 5-, 3-irons and wood clubs.

**3. Plane Creation.** Create an image of your personal swing plane. Make it steel or cloth or plastic or even a laser light—whatever you like. Then practice hitting balls so that your downswing plane lies on or beneath this creation.

☐☐**Pace, Pace, Pace**

**1. Slow-motion Exercise.** Hit balls with first a 7-iron and then a 3-wood or driver, attempting to hit the ball half your normal distance with that club. Make each swing a full swing, but keep the distance to half. Notice how easy it is to maintain path and plane.

**2. Pace Drill Review.** Go back and find your favorite swing-speed exercise and do it again now while swinging a 7-iron. Find a pace that allows you to keep the club on proper path and plane. Learn to associate speed with timing. Note what happens to your ball-flight when you speed up or slow down.

☐☐**Mind Games**

1. Play a "round" on the practice range.
2. Play a "round" at home.

# 10

# TAKING IT TO THE COURSE

Let's return for a moment to the playground and the little girl on the swing. Sit back down on your park bench and watch her play and, as you do, add children to the picture. Fill all the seats on the swings, pack the merry-go-round and the sandbox and have a line of children waiting to slide down the slide. Listen to the noise those happy children are making, the excitement they bring to these simple activities. Think of the fun they're having just playing.

Now contrast that picture of fun with the last hole-by-hole description you got from one of your friends about his or her golf game. Did it sound like fun in the way those children were having fun? Or did it sound like work? As teachers we see the excitement of players who have cured a slice or straightened out a perpetual hook. We watch their faces light up as they hit "career" shots on the practice range. They can't wait to call us down the practice line and show us their new swings. They're like those kids in the park. The third and fourth days of our golf schools are filled with shouts from students: "Bob! Davis! You won't believe the 3-wood I just hit. Wow!!"

Unfortunately, the success only occasionally carries over to the golf course, and the excitement rarely does. Folks get so darn serious on the golf course, you'd think they had to make a living at it. And Bob Rotella, the psychologist who's written our chapter on relaxation (page 136) tells us the tour pros have the same problem. Once we're out on the course, all of us who work hard at our games so that we'll play well and enjoy it more, often forget to PLAY—and forget to ENJOY. If you step from the range to the first tee and keep WORKING, you miss all the fun.

It will be your ability to relax and enjoy yourself, to just plain play, that will enhance your ability to improve. Isn't that ironic? Unless you can let go and have fun on the course, you won't trust the work you've done before you got there. And without that relaxed trust, the work is for nought.

The Scots are never given enough credit for separating "practice field" from "golf course." That separation was brilliant. We know the difference well in other parts of our life. We know that we get off work at 5 p.m., and we have a different attitude as we drive home from work and decide what we're going to do for recreation. There is anticipation, excitement. In golf, as in most motor-skill sports, the only reason for practice is to enjoy the play more. If I haven't practiced I have to think about my swing when I get on the course. So I have to work. But when I'm prepared I move quickly into the "play" environment. I hit my shot, watch it land and know I can find it. Then I can walk down the fairway "on vacation." That's a lot more fun than walking along thinking, "I must remember to keep that right elbow tucked in a little more. . . ." That's not fun at all, that's work. It's not trusting oneself, it's prodding oneself. It's like playing golf with a screaming back-seat driver walking right behind you all day.

***Back-seat driver***
*Taking loads of mechanical thoughts with you onto the course is like inviting a back-seat driver. It takes the fun out of your game and undermines your swing.*

Peter Thomson, the five-time British Open champion and Senior PGA Tour star, said: "It's a good idea to make up your mind to like a course you are about to play, to like the people you are playing with and to enjoy the weather, hot or cold." Your first tip on taking your new swing on the course, therefore, is to decide to enjoy the experience.

But how do you take advantage of the playful state of mind Peter speaks of? How do you further put your mind at ease so your body can perform? Here are some of the ways.

## Preparation and warm-up

As we said in the last chapter, the time to practice is after the round. What you do before a round is warm up. The difference? Before a round you're not trying to mold or fix your swing, you're trying to discover it. What's my swing today? Am I hooking the ball or am I fading it? What's my tendency? Am I aligning myself correctly? Do I feel strong, or will I need an extra club? How is the temperature affecting the ball's flight? What is the ball doing after it lands? What kind of spin does it have? How hard or soft is the practice-range ground? Is there any reason to think the course will be different? If so, how?

Discover, don't make demands of your swing before a round. And then, as Sam Snead said, "Dance with the one what brung ya'."

This pre-play time is when your course awareness begins, too. After hitting some balls to get the feel of your swing, make chips from different lies around the practice green. Watch how the ball runs or bites. How does it fly from short grass? Tall? What chipping club do you seem to have the best feel with from each of the lies?

Make putts from various distances to get the feel for the speed of the green. Be prepared for a slightly different speed on the course, but be observant on the practice green. If you have only a little time, start with putts of three feet and don't move any farther away until you are making most of those. Work out in half-foot increments to six feet.

Some players like to begin with putting and then move to the practice tee and finish with the club they'll use on the first tee. That's fine. Or give yourself enough time to hit a few balls, make some chips and putts and then go back to the tee to hit the club you'll use to tee off.

Whatever order you choose, remember that this is a time for learning, not working. Don't force a swing change or try to make a fix 15 minutes before your round. It won't take.

If you finish your regular practice sessions by playing a few holes and chipping extra balls around each of the greens you play, the transition from range to course will be easier when you come to play a regular 18. Don't beat balls every night after work and then show up on Saturday and play your first hole of the week. Try to make moving from practice tee to first tee a regular part of your practice.

## "Feeling" the course

The practice tee is the place to get the feel for your golf swing. On the course, you must get a feel for the course. Preoccupation with swing mechanics, or even with your own emotional state, makes feeling the course impossible.

Getting a feel for the course means being observant. It means getting to know the hardness or softness of the greens, how firm the fairways are, how much a ball is going to run and which way it's going to kick after it hits. When you're enjoying the game, you take it all in. You're interested in all shots, even mis-hits, because they are giving you feedback. If you're pulling the ball today, then pay attention to its flight so that you know exactly how much you're pulling it—and play for it. That's how a player—as opposed to a practicer—thinks.

***Be observant***
*Getting the feel of a course begins with observing it. Watching how all your shots—good or bad—fly, roll and kick will help you on upcoming holes. Take in everything.*

You'll make the transition from practice to play easier with a consistent preshot routine. A routine is the procedure you go through just prior to hitting a shot. You want your routine to be the same from one shot to the next. You want it to take the same amount of time. You want it to include the same alignment procedure each time. That breeds consistency. Some players' routines include a practice swing, some don't. Most "waggle" the club just before swinging. Some do it once, some more than once. The point is, keep your routine consistent so that the swing that follows it will be consistent, too.

One key choice you have in designing a routine is how you'll approach the ball. Some players walk to the address position from behind the ball, along the target line. Others approach the ball at a 90-degree angle from the target line. Experiment to find which of these approaches helps you get aligned to feel your proper swing path most easily.

There is only one hard-and-fast rule about routines: Go through your routine at the same pace you want to swing. If your swing pace is naturally brisk, make your routine brisk also. If you want your tempo to be slow, let your routine reflect that.

A routine combats the temptation to go through a checklist to cover before every shot—ball position here, left arm here, head down, weight forward, knees flexed. . . . With every item, another part of the body moves for a moment. By the time you get on the course, these things need to be automatic. Work on your preshot routine on the practice range so that on the course things like ball position and posture occur naturally. That way you can be concerned about club selection, good tempo and target. A routine makes correct fundamentals automatic, giving you a chance to play—really PLAY—on the course.

## Every swing a distance swing

Getting a feel for the course means getting a feel for distance. Distance control, unfortunately, is the bane of most amateurs' games. They use directional targets, but seldom calculate the precise distance they have to hit the ball. Off the tee, for example, they may aim at a landmark such as a pole or steeple, but rarely can they tell you how far they want the ball to go. Few know how far they hit each club, and most ignore or underestimate climatic or topographical factors affecting distance. In his book, *Bobby Jones on Golf,*

Jones said, "The average golfer has not the faculty . . . of quickly sizing up the requirements of a golf shot and of choosing the club and the method of playing it . . . To conquer an unfamiliar layout, considerable work must be done by what lies between the golfer's ears."

Have a precise distance in mind on every swing you make and have a feel for the swing speed you need for that distance. It is not enough to say, "This is about a 6-iron." For example, let's say you've driven the ball to the 150-yard marker. The pin is in the middle of the green and that's where the marker is measured from—no additional yardage there. You usually hit a 6-iron 150 yards. But you're not done yet—there are other factors to consider. Let's go through your thought process: "It is 150 yards, but the wind is in my face, so now it is 160 yards. The lie is sitting up on some really firm-looking turf and there is not much grass or sponginess in there, so that should neither add nor subtract yardage. Still 160. The green is above me, elevated about 20 feet, so now my yardage is 165 yards. Now I'm ready to hit. It's not a 6-iron anymore. I'll hit the 5." You choose your target—perhaps a shadow on the green close to the pin or the pin itself—and take your aim.

But there's one more step. Once you have taken your aim and your address you've done everything you can to control the quality of your swing. Now you're on automatic pilot. You've worked hard on the range. You've determined how far you hit your clubs. You've developed a routine to assure proper alignment. You're as ready as you can be. The one remaining factor is swing speed. If you can't control the speed of your swing, no degree of technical ability can save you on the course. So once you step on the course, pace is the factor that most determines the quality of your performance. What does pace have to do with distance control? Pace is a slave to uncertainty and tension, and if there is any doubt in your mind as you step up to the ball, you'll find it impossible to swing at the pace you wish. So the last step, as you address the ball, is to have that number sitting in the front of your mind as you make your swing: 165 yards. Your mind is a marvelous machine when you give it specific information and it will get the word to your arms and legs and hands and feet and together they'll give you the 165-yard 5-iron swing. Davis says that until he began *thinking* a specific distance on each swing he couldn't feel the swing speed he needed. He tended to swing too hard on most shots—a common mistake among weekend players. That's understandable, because when you give your mind imprecise information—"It's about a 6-iron"—and it knows there's a 10 m.p.h. wind blowing, the green's elevated and you've selected a 6-iron, it will say to the rest of your body, "Boys, we're going to have to wail and flail with this club to get the ball there." You know the rest. Arrive at a specific distance, select a club that can send the ball that distance with an easy swing, and then keep that distance in your mind as you make that easy swing.

In general, add 10 yards for every 10 m.p.h. of wind and every 15 feet of elevation. Add five yards if the lie is bare and subtract five if the lie is fluffy. Add 10 yards when the temperature dips below 50.

All this depends, of course, on knowing the yardage. For some reason a lot golfers find the calculation of yardage a dull task and won't do it even if it means walking only 12 or 15 yards from their ball to a marker. It also depends on knowing how far you hit each club, something that doesn't take a whole day or an empty golf course to find out. The easiest way is to keep a scorecard or note pad in your back pocket and anytime you hit a good, solid shot with any club, have your partner drive the cart while you pace it off. Put the yardage in your notebook and before too long you've got all your clubs recorded.

For those of you with a bit more time and ambition, chart your shot-dispersion patterns. On an empty fairway or the range at the end of the day, hit 25 balls with one club and

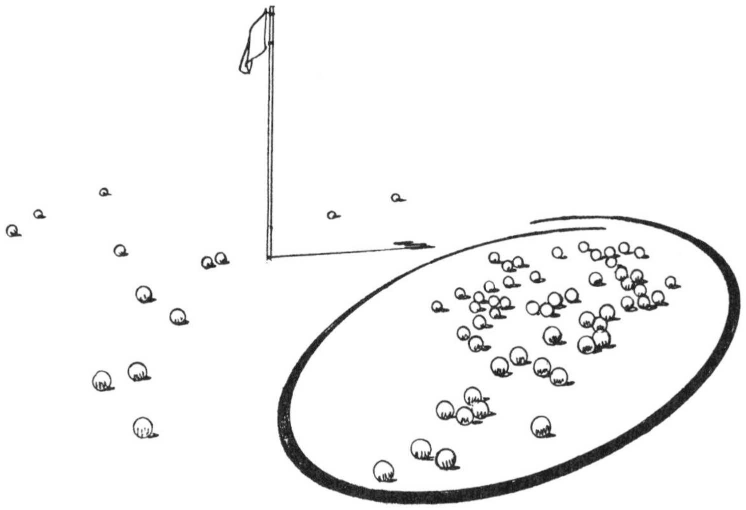

***Shot patterns***
*On a practice range or field, chart your shot dispersion pattern with different clubs. Know how far you hit each club with an average shot, which side of your target you tend to miss on.*

then pace off the width and depth of the shot pattern, throwing out the occasional "foul ball." On the course take that pattern into consideration. If your very best 7-iron is 152 and you've got 150 yards with a deep bunker fronting the green, obviously you want the 6. If the bunker is right and your pattern is off-center to the right, you'll want to compensate by aiming slightly left. If there's out-of-bounds behind the green and you know you've hit a few 7-irons 165 yards, you might want to drop down a club.

A note about caddies. One of the benefits of learning the game when Bob and Davis did was caddieing and later using caddies as players. The golf cart has done wonderful things for the growth of the game, but it has for the most part made the caddie obsolete and that's too bad. A caddie is the extra pair of eyes and ears, the extra bundle of experience, that can help you know the course better. He or she can help with distances. He can tell you where the architect

***Caddies***
*A caddie is your extra pair of ears and eyes. When you have the chance, take one. Do what you can at your club or course to foster a caddie program.*

has played a trick by placing a bunker that looks like it's greenside, but is 10 or 20 yards forward of that. He can get to know you and help you make sensible club selections. He can encourage you and help you stay composed, and as Bob's old Scottish friend Jimmy McCormick used to do for Bob, tell you, "Me lad, you're swinging well and you're in balance today," or "You're not swinging well and you're not a bit in balance." There are some areas of the country, such as the Chicago district, where caddies are still plentiful. We would encourage you to use a caddie whenever you have a chance, and to do what you can to build the caddie population at your club. Believe us, it will help your game.

## Enemy No. 1: Tension

Physical tension is the ruination of more on-course swings among both amateurs and professionals than any other single cause. It may result from indecision, from pressure, from excitement, from your perception about what other players are thinking or saying about you. The night before he was to play the final round of the 1986 British Open, leader Greg Norman was paid a visit at dinner by Jack Nicklaus. It was Nicklaus, remember, who had "stolen" a major from Norman four months before when Nicklaus won his sixth Masters and Norman, on his final approach shot, hit the ball wildly and bogeyed the 18th hole. Now Nicklaus had come to wish Norman good luck and give him a little piece of advice in the Australian's quest for his first major. "He told me to monitor my grip pressure," said Norman. Grip pressure! Who would have thought that "monitor your grip pressure" would be the "secret" passed between these two great players on the eve of the British Open. And yet it's superb advice whether you're playing a friendly nassau at your club or attempting to qualify for the U. S. Amateur. Your hands will reveal the first signs of tension, and from your hands tension will spread to your arms, your shoulders, your lower body.

Attitude and emotional control play a large role in controlling tension and in a moment we will talk about them. First, here's an exercise from Davis' colleague at Sea Island, Ga., Jimmy Hodges, that's great for checking grip tension. Swing a club back and forth without stopping until you can get the clubhead to feel as heavy as possible. It may take a little time, but you'll notice that you have to decrease grip pressure to begin to feel that clubhead. After it's feeling

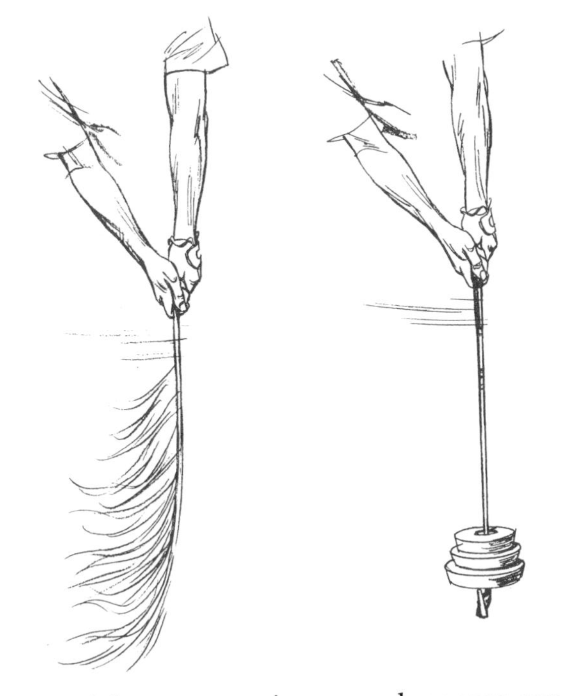

***Feather test***
*Check grip tension by swinging a club back and forth until you can make the head feel as heavy as possible, as heavy as a barbell. Then tighten your grip and feel the clubhead turn into a feather—a feather you can't control.*

very heavy, tighten your grip as much as you can. Notice how the heaviness disappears.

## Pace, pace, pace

We spoke earlier of the relationship between distance control and swing speed. We come back to pace now because it encompasses more than simply the speed of your swing. Granted, it begins with that. We want you to swing as fast as you can while maintaining balance, i.e., to swing within yourself. Dan Pohl, one of the PGA Tour's longest hitters, said recently that he began to win on tour when he slowed his swing pace down to "80 or 85 percent" of maximum, because that lesser speed made him more accurate. Notice that Pohl didn't say he made his swing shorter. He already had one of the shortest backswings on tour and it still is very short. But before it was short and fast; now it is short and under control. It's not swing length that destroys most amateurs' tempo; it's swing speed.

A great model of pace and tempo is Fuzzy Zoeller. All of us can't have Fuzzy's sense of humor on the course, but we can emulate his relaxed manner and his graceful pace. At the other end of the swing-pace spectrum is Arnold Palmer, a great player and a great man, but not someone we'd recommend as a model of pace. Arnold is one of the few players in the world who can go at the ball with the force and speed he does. That pace works for him and him alone because of his tremendous hand and forearm strength. He's got the power to return the clubhead squarely to the ball while still swinging as hard as he does. Few others can, and we don't recommend that you try. Unfortunately, many amateurs have modeled themselves after charismatic Arnie, and paid the price of an inappropriate swing pace. To find the pace that best combines speed and control, make swings with your eyes closed. You'll naturally swing at a speed that allows you to stay in balance, allowing the club to swing freely.

## Rehearsal swing

One of the keys to maintaining good pace is your rehearsal or preparatory swing. We don't like the term practice swing much because it conjures up a practice range and a bucket of balls. Your rehearsal swing is not a practice stroke. Practice time is over. It's your way of establishing the pace—and path—of the swing you're about to make without worrying about club-ball contact. As you make this preparatory swing you're thinking about the speed of your swing and the path of the clubhead, so that by the time you address the ball, you've programmed yourself to repeat that automatically. Now you can concentrate on target. Watch your playing partners. See how often the player who loses his tempo has become sloppy with that preparatory swing.

But proper pace is not entirely a mechanical thing. On the day of a round, your whole day is pace. Pace is how fast or slow you drive to the course, hit practice balls, walk between shots. It is your routine as you choose a club and set up to shoot. All of these things bear on the pace of your swing.

## Concentration, confidence, composure

We spoke of the three "Ps"—Practice, Perseverance and Patience—in the Putting-It-Together Chapter. On the course, it's the three "Cs"—Concentration, Confidence and Composure. The first of these is frequently misunderstood. Chuck Hogan, who advises many tour players on the "mental side," says most players think concentration means "blocking out" when it really means "taking in." If you think of concentrating as knitting your brow and trying to insulate yourself from the sounds and smells and feelings you have on the course, that's not it. In fact, according to Hogan, it's the opposite. It's letting those stimuli in, letting them help you prepare for your shot. You've heard people say that under great stress—during a fire or an automobile accident, for example—they experienced things in "slow motion" and felt and saw things more vividly than normal. Their accounts are the very opposite of what we have come to think of as concentration—a kind of blocking out of sensation—and yet they were concentrating perfectly. Their lives were at stake. Athletes report the same kind of experience when they talk about "being in the zone." Halfbacks will tell you that they see holes in the line almost before they appear. Tennis players and baseball hitters say the ball seems to get bigger. Golfers report a total lack of effort, an automaticity in their swings, a sense of oneness with the course.

The lesson is, don't block things out. Let things in on the course. Don't fight the sights and sounds around you. Let them in, listen to them quietly and let them help you get to know the course, the fairway, the greens better. Blocking out takes tremendous energy and you certainly can't do it for four hours. Enjoy the course, enjoy the round and concentrating will be easier. As it comes time to hit a shot, narrow your focus to your target, your routine and your swing tempo. Then broaden your focus again and let the lay of the land, the shape of bunkers, the feel of the wind, even the smell of the grass help you instinctively prepare for the next shot.

That kind of concentration makes maintaining your composure and poise much easier. "Proper poise is everything," wrote Seymour Dunn. "Without correct poise there can be no good results." Having poise and composure means being prepared for the good and the bad and maintaining emotional control no matter what happens. That does not mean eliminating all emotion on the course. Seve Ballesteros is a very emotional golfer who has marvelous composure. From the moment he strikes his golf ball, you know if he is happy or disappointed. But his glee at a great shot and his disappointment at a poor one are always in control. There is another shot to hit and Seve strides to it with purpose and pride. No one shot will ever make or defeat him.

Keeping your composure will be easier, reaching your potential will be possible, if you separate your self-worth from how you play the game. Great players don't equate "I am a good player or I am a bad player" with "I am a good person or I am a bad person." They play for the enjoyment of playing and if they play well they simply enjoy it more. Their scores do not control their attitudes. Their attitudes control their scores. Think about other sports and games you play. You don't judge yourself a terrible person if you go fishing and fail to catch anything. Davis kids his son, Mark, about being the worst fisherman in the world because he seldom catches any fish, but Mark loves fishing. You can see the anticipation in his face as he gets his gear ready, packs his lunch and heads for the water. Catching fish would be nice but it's secondary to the enjoyment of the experience. The hard truth about the game of golf is that you are bound to hit more bad shots than good. What's more, it's an unpredictable game, with bad and good breaks often determining whether you meet your scoring goal or not. Acknowledge that before you start so you can put your mind at ease—then your body can perform and you are apt to make the fewest mistakes possible. The players with great poise, players like Seve and Nicklaus, are people who seem to get stronger when things get worse. It is easy to be composed when things are going great. But when things are going badly it takes strength, courage and the perception that no matter what happens, "I can cope."

We're not recommending, however, that you fake composure on the course or pretend to be poised. Faking it makes it worse. If you're of the Craig Stadler mold you're better off blowing your top and getting it over with than you would be holding it in to look "poised." Composure is an attitude you have embraced rather than an appearance you have adopted.

Bob is fond of saying that exposure creates composure. But it takes time. Seek out golfing situations that challenge you. Perhaps it's a little bigger bet than you ordinarily make. Perhaps it's more tournament play. Maybe it's playing with players who are better than you are. Expose yourself to a more competitive environment and you'll learn to stay composed in it.

Confidence is the third leg of our on-course tripod. We'd like to address a major misconception about it among the weekend players we see. What they call confidence is really overconfidence. Saying, for example, "I'm going to win today." Or "I'm going to break par today," or even "I'm going to break 100 today" is not confidence. That's dumb, frankly, because it raises your expectations and sets you up for disappointment, frustration and a loss of poise. Confidence is saying, "It's possible for me to play great today. I'm prepared. I've practiced. And I'm going to give it my best shot. But that's all I can control." Or "It's possible for me to hit this shot the way I'd like to. I've got the ability and I'm prepared. I'm going to do my best." Then, let go and see what happens. That's not selling out; that's real confidence, and it will go a lot farther than bravado.

Both Bob and Davis are basketball fans and the great UCLA basketball coach John Wooden has given us a fitting comment with which to end this chapter. Wooden won a record 10 national championships during his tenure at UCLA. And yet he says, "In 27 years, I never once talked about winning. Instead, I would tell my players before the game, 'When it is over I want your heads up. And there is only one way your heads can be up. That's for you to know, not me, that you gave the best effort of which you are capable. If you do that, then the score really doesn't matter. Although I have a feeling that if you do that the score will be to your liking.' I honestly, deeply believe that in not stressing winning as such we won more than we would have if I had stressed outscoring opponents."

Doing your best can be accomplished every time you go out on the course. Winning your match or breaking par or breaking 100 can't be. Remember, when things go awry on the course, it's the chance to compete that you came for, not the result. It's the chance to do your best that excited you, not a particular score. "Why do so many people dread adversity," says Wooden, "when it is only through adversity that we grow stronger?" If you can remember that, as Coach Wooden says, the score will probably be to your liking.

## Your Game Plan

1. Play a round with John Wooden's words in mind. Think only of walking off the course at the end of the day "with your head up." Do your best on each shot, enjoy the day and the surroundings and let the score take care of itself.

2. During a round, monitor only your distance control. Did you have a specific distance in mind on every shot? How close did your shot finish to that distance?

3. Review a round solely on the basis of emotional control and stability. Were you able to maintain your poise during the round? Under what circumstances did you lose it? What type of shot or situation caused you more anxiety than any other?

4. Play a round, monitoring your grip pressure on every single shot. Don't worry about score. What kind of a round was it? How did your swing feel that day?

▽ ▽ ▽ ▽ ▽ ▽ ▽ ▽ ▽ ▽

# AFTERWORD

# FEELING YOUR MIND AND BODY

## BY DR. ROBERT ROTELLA

Feeling your body as you swing a golf club requires relaxation. If you are not relaxed, your muscles tense and the swing you have worked so hard to shape is lost. Enjoying the game also requires that you be relaxed. If you are always scrutinizing your performance, judging yourself, allowing your feelings about yourself to be based on your score, there will be little fun in the game for you. When the mind is full of judgments, the body will respond with tension. Not only won't you enjoy yourself, you won't play as well as you are capable of playing.

In a moment, I will offer a relaxation technique you can use on a daily basis. But it would be unfair to suggest that a technique alone can alter the way you feel, or how you feel about your golf game. Physical relations begin with your lifestyle and your outlook on life. In a culture as imbued with the work ethic as ours, that may mean you'll have to reexamine the way you think about all of your life, not just your golf game.

### Two styles of thinking

Most high-achieving adults spend their time primarily in a "training" mind-set. They analyze their performances. They "try" to get better. They "work" at life. They typically need to learn to trust their abilities more. "Train" and "trust" are two very different mentalities. Rather than looking at one as good and the other as bad, let's examine why it is appropriate to use one or the other. The ideal is to learn how to blend the two rather than falling in love with one or the other, as is often the case.

## Training

The training mind-set involves making a conscious effort to take control over your life. The calling cards of this mind-set are intentionally trying hard, making it happen, taking charge, willfully producing intensity, desire and forced effort. This style of thinking is dominated by judgment, evaluation, analysis and criticism. When you're in the training mind-set, you're "working on" your weaknesses. It is an active mindset, often filled with anticipation of future problems, challenges and flaws.

The worry and concern of the training mind-set are great motivators in the workplace and on the practice tee. But eventually it works against you in your career. And for enjoying leisure time, interacting with your family or playing golf it is most detrimental.

Besides often bringing success at work and technical efficiency in the tasks you undertake, the training mind-set also assures regular pats on the back. You will probably be praised for your attitude even if, "despite trying so hard," you fail. Rewards like this cause many high-achieving adults to get stuck in attitudes that look good and sound good but don't work. They're left with the feeling that they have "a great attitude." But not necessarily results.

After at first providing great motivation and a large amount of success, this mind-set eventually prevents further success and happiness. It leads to a build up of stress. Gradually the opportunities you worked so hard to achieve become a burden. You take on more than you can handle. You notice that you can't do everything you promised despite stretching your days to the breaking point. Despite feeling the need to back off a bit, you can't stand the thought of doing it. You've worked too hard for your success to risk losing everything you've obtained. Your guilt tells you to watch out: You may be getting lazy or complacent. Or you worry about letting others down. Your continued striving is for them, not for yourself.

At the same time, you feel uneasy anytime you're not the best at what you do and fear that others are gaining on you. To stay motivated, you keep thinking of your flaws and failures. You set more and more perfectionistic standards that you can't possibly obtain.

What's happened? You've become more and more serious. You've lost your spontaneity. This is a typical and natural result of spending most of your waking hours in the training mentality. We're all victims of habit and as we grow comfortable with this way of thinking, it comes to control and dominate our lives. We are lost without a regular fix of several hours of "training." It has now become virtually impossible to relax, even when on vacation or while out playing golf.

The question is: Can you feel what your mind and body are trying to tell you? Will you listen to them? It's time to change.

## Trusting and letting go

A trusting mind-set involves letting go of the continual effort to control all elements of your life. It consists of allowing yourself simply to enjoy the feeling of experiences and to respond to them without any conscious attempt to second-guess, judge or critique your feelings. It's the opposite of the training mentality, which hesitates to undertake new experiences for fear of making mistakes. The trusting mind-set has room for pure feeling, a quiet mood and spontaneity. It urges you to listen to your feelings and your body (which is why it's a boon to your golf game).

If you're lost in the training mind-set, people will tell you that you never relax, that you're uptight. You "know" they're wrong. Your golf professional tells you that you are too tight or too tense to swing. You don't understand it or don't want to hear it. You resist. Eventually your physician tells you your blood pressure is high or you are hypertensive. You're convinced he's wrong. You've always had total control over your life. How can this be happening?

Deep down you know the truth. You realize it's time for a change. But how do you let go? How do you get into the trusting mind-set? First, you must be willing to discard some habits, such as constantly planning, analyzing and preparing for tomorrow. It's time to trust yourself to know how to have success without consciously trying to *make it happen.* You must let yourself enjoy the feeling of a passive mind-set—and that will seem strange at first. It will feel like complacency, even laziness. But that's the price of experiencing the rest of the American Dream—enjoyment, relaxation and, in this case, a golf game based on natural ability and feel, not on effort. The time has come to blend the training and trusting mind-set.

That blending begins with self-awareness. It means listening to your body, acknowledging your true feelings about your work and your relationships. It means remembering that long-term success includes health and family life, not just career. Many people who look like they are successful are very unhappy and sometimes unhealthy. What are you feeling, really?

Trusting means changing old work habits. Don't let the overwork you used to get your career off the ground become a lifelong habit. Make the transition to working less, with increased quality gained from experience. Make the commitment to stop working when you leave the office. Bringing work home with you and thinking about work at home help in the early stages of your career. But it's time now to draw clear lines between work and recreation. If you don't, recreation will become work.

Slow down. The only way to eliminate impatience and anger is to slow down and enjoy life more. Learn to eat more slowly, drive more slowly, talk more slowly, listen better.

Allow spontaneous, spur-of-the-moment activities back in your highly structured life. Take at least one day a week or the weekend for recreation or for doing whatever you feel like. Let go. During this time, start and stop activities as you feel like it. Quit fighting the clock. Get back to hobbies and recreational activities you once enjoyed and gave up. Do them with friends rather than work associates—or at least refuse to use this time to discuss business.

Make your expectations honest. With all of your recreation, and especially with golf, make certain your goals are in line with the amount of time you're able to allot.

Finally, acknowledge that "I'm OK—you're OK." When you leave work, take off the competitive armor. Let the other fellow do it his way, you do it your way, and be grateful that people are unique. What a bore life would be if we were all the same!

## Relaxation through autogenic training

Autogenic training is a relaxation technique developed by the German psychiatrist Johannes Schultz in 1932 to create the body warmth and heaviness usually associated with hypnosis. Auto means "self-administered," genic, "for a healthful purpose." The warmth occurs as a result of blood vessel dilation, the heaviness due to muscles relaxing. Autogenic training can help you decrease your heart and respiration rates, muscle tension and cholesterol level while increasing your meditative alpha brain waves as well as the blood flow to your arms and legs. In some cases regular practice has alleviated migraine headaches, insomnia and high blood pressure.

Autogenic training uses the sensations of heaviness and warmth to relax the body, then extends this relaxed state to the mind by means of imagery. Its effectiveness depends on daily practice. Don't allow yourself excuses for not doing it. You have the time if health, happiness and success are priorities. And if those reasons are not enough, do it for the good of your golf game.

The basic technique follows. Do the exercises and accept whatever happens. Do not try to make something happen. That won't help.

It's best to recline, but you may also sit in a chair or on a stool with your forearms resting on your thighs. Do the training twice daily for about 20 minutes each time. The training requires that you use the specific phrases below. Memorize them, have someone read them to you, or record them, perhaps over the sounds of the sea or of a soft flute or guitar. Whatever your method, the words must be spoken with a calm, soft voice, with pauses sufficient for you to bring about the desired sensations.

Begin by taking your chosen position in a quiet and comfortable environment. Repeat or listen to these phrases:

I am calm.
It is quiet.
I am relaxed.
My right arm (if right-handed) is heavy.
 (Repeat this phrase five times.)
My right arm is warm.
 (Repeat five times.)
My right arm is tingly.
My right arm is heavy and warm.

My right arm is weighted down and feels warm.
My left arm is heavy.
(Repeat five times.)
My left arm is warm.
(Repeat five times.)
My left arm is tingly.
My left arm is heavy and warm.
My left arm is weighted down and feels warm.
Both my arms are heavy and warm.
(Repeat five times.)
My right leg is heavy.
(Repeat five times.)
My right leg is warm.
(Repeat five times.)
My right leg is tingly.
My right leg is heavy and warm.
My right leg is weighted down and feels warm.
My left leg is heavy.
(Repeat five times.)
My left leg is warm.
(Repeat five times.)
My left leg is tingly.
My left leg is heavy and warm.
My left leg is weighted down and warm.
Both my legs feel heavy and warm.
(Repeat five times.)
My heart is beating calmly.
I am relaxed.
My heart is calm and relaxed.
(Repeat five times.)
My breathing is regular.
My breathing is calm.
My breathing is calm and relaxed.
(Repeat five times.)
My solar plexus is warm.
(Repeat five times.)
I feel warmth throughout my abdomen.
(Repeat five times.)
My forehead is cool.
(Repeat five times.)
I am calm.
I am relaxed.
I am quiet.

Now think of a relaxing scene, a place where you almost always find it easy to be relaxed.
Imagine yourself there.
See this scene clearly.
Experience it.
Enjoy how good it feels.
Hear the sounds.
See the colors.
This scene relaxes you.
You are calm.
You are quiet.
You are at peace.
Your mind is quiet.
Your whole body is quiet, heavy, warm and relaxed.
Your thoughts are of your quiet, heavy, warm body and of your scene.
Tell yourself you feel quiet, you feel relaxed, you feel calm.
Now prepare to leave your scene.
Count backwards from five.
With each number you will be closer to opening your eyes.
Five.
You are leaving your scene.
Four.
You are back in this room.
You are reclining (or seated).
You know where you are.
Three.
Prepare to open your eyes.
Think of what you will see when you open your eyes.
Two.
Open your eyes.
Focus upon one object in the room.
Take a deep breath.
One.

Bob and Davis have said that tension is your greatest enemy. Doing this relaxation exercise will help you defeat that enemy. It will help you enjoy the game more as you establish and feel the rhythm of your golf swing.